LOVE
YOUR
84,000
HOURS
AT WORK

*Stories on the Road from People
with Purpose and Passion*

ANDREW HARRISON

DOTTED
LINES PRESS

Love Your 84,000 Hours at Work

ISBN: 978-0-9826700-0-2

This book was printed in the United States of America
Published by Dotted Lines Press

For my parents,
whose unending moral support
has shown me time and again
what unconditional love is all about.

For my fellow Seekers:
On the road, there will be ups and downs;
to live your dreams, you can't give up.
Purpose, passion and perseverance
will get you where you are meant to go.

CONTENTS

CONTENTS

CONTENTS

ACKNOWLEDGEMENTS

It has been a long journey to make this book a reality. Multitudes assisted me on my road. I am sincerely sorry that I can't list every individual.

First off, I need to thank God for bringing such eye-opening people, places and experiences into my life. I may not always let You know it, but I feel truly blessed to be where I am today. You probably chuckle sometimes at my stubbornness and my desire to control my destiny, but please, keep guiding me. I realize You've made me for a reason and it seems as though we have a lot more work to do.

Without my interviewees, there would be no book. Whether you are in the book or not, your story shaped me. Thank you for talking with me and letting me to get to know you.

To my parents, there is a reason you are on the dedication page. I am ecstatic to finally have this book to share with you. It's been a long road and you have always been there for me. Thanks for reading the chapters in their infancy, for picking me up when I was ready to quit, and most of all, for your love. I love you.

Thanks to my brother Brad, sister Caytie and brother-in-law Bryan for your support and for putting up with my quirks. To my Uncle Bill Reddy, your continued belief in me has been a great propellant. To my older cousins Kevin and Colin, thanks for taking an interest in me and my view of the world. Rave on.

I also appreciate guidance from Jennifer Sertl, my initial coach. Thanks for your confidence in me and getting through my thick-headedness. Brian Koval, thanks for reaching out to me and then for being there when I was questioning my purpose.

All of my hosts on the road showed me incredible hospitality. It would have been a lonely time going from city to city by myself, so thank you for opening your homes to me. I enjoyed the camaraderie, the sightseeing, and of course, the meals.

To all of the people who said, "I know someone you should interview," thank you.

Media outlets who initially decided my story was worth sharing showed me that I had to pay the lessons of my journey forward. Thanks to Ashley Fantz and Scott Andron of the *Miami Herald*, Peter St. Onge of the *Charlotte Observer*, and Kevin Salwen of *Worthwhile Magazine*.

To the authors who have fielded my questions, thank you so much. Sandra Beckwith, you have been a huge help every step of the way. Randi Minetor, I appreciate your advice. Paul Vitale, your positive energy is contagious.

I have had great help with all aspects of publication and electronic media. To my editor, Wendy Low, you were great to work with. Julie Russell, thanks for your input on those preliminary chapters. To my proofreaders Mary Ann Giglio and Barbara Kennedy, thank you for your attention to detail. To Nancy Ciolek, for laying out the book. To Allison Shirreffs, for the picture on the back cover. To Doug Wood, for getting IamOnTheRoad.com off the ground. To Bobby Blake, for turning the site into what it has become. To Chuck Duncan, for working with me on 8400hours.com. To Mike Picciotti and Matt Miller, for your help on my videos. And to Nicole Corea, for your vision and creation of the book cover and website.

All the friends who reinforced my vision deserve my deep thanks. To Carol Dombrose and Chris Reynolds of Angel House in Strongsville, Ohio, thanks for a special place. I am glad our paths continue to cross. To Angelo Piccone, our lunches have given me confidence. To Scott Lindenberg, our talks and your recommendations have helped form my road. To Bob Rosenfeld, our working together has caused me to grow professionally, socially and spiritually. And to Mark Cuban: you were right. "It's easy to ask for cash. It's hard to have the nuts to do it on your own."

To the places that have educated me, thank you. At the University of Arkansas at Little Rock, Dr. Chuck Anderson showed me I might have what it takes to write. My Kappa Sigma Fraternity brothers taught me that common bonds cement friendships for life. The University of South Carolina opened my eyes to how powerful a tool communication can be. And I learned a lot from my St. John Fisher College students, including that being called professor could be a fit later in my career.

To everyone else I have encountered on my road up to this point, in one way or another, you have had an influence on me, and though I cannot mention each and every one of you, I thank you.

And now, as you embark on my book, my thanks go to you—the reader.

Finding What Was Missing

For the first 28 years of my life I did what I was supposed to do. I followed what society expected of me and other people's ideas of what would make me happy. And it was a great way to live. I had a loving family, many friends, undergraduate and master's degrees, a new car, new clothes, an apartment in the heart of a growing metropolis and a career that provided stability and enough money to live very comfortably. But it was also a life that left me feeling like there was something missing. I didn't know what was missing, I just knew I wasn't happy with the life I was living.

And I'll tell you, it's a puzzling, strange and unnerving feeling when you attain your goals and are still left unfulfilled. I tried different ways to "escape" my dilemma. While some of the escapes were good, some were not so good. The lack of fulfillment eventually spurred me to ask a lot of hard questions about myself, my work and my existence.

At the age of 28, I decided I wasn't going to wait for the answers to my questions to fall from the sky. I was going to seek out the answers and find my purpose in life. It was a decision that I wrestled with for many months. It was a decision that both frightened and energized me. It was a decision that caused my family to freak out, my friends to wonder what was wrong with me and my employer to send me to an industrial psychologist.

My decision was to quit a stable job that would pay me $100,000 a year while typically working less than 40 hours per week. My decision was to cash in my life savings to travel the United States interviewing people who had what I lacked: passion for their work and life.

What has transpired since the last day at my job has changed me forever. I've traveled over 75,000 miles and conducted over 145 interviews with people from all walks of life. The people I've met showed me that, without question, there are people who work and live with passion. They told me about their personal journeys and gave me advice for people who were struggling like I was. They helped me find the answers to my questions.

As my journey evolved, I realized there were many other people wrestling with the same life questions that I was asking myself. Word of mouth about my journey and website spread rapidly. Strangers emailed to wish me well, to offer food and lodging or to recommend someone I should interview. Media outlets contacted me to get stories on the journey. And due to that exposure, various groups asked me to give talks about what I'd learned.

Since going on the road, I know my initial decision was a risk that had to be taken. Now, I can't imagine my life any other way. I found my purpose in the journey—to help everyone have the same passion for their work and for their life that my interview subjects, and now I, have.

Not everyone can look for their answers by quitting their job and cashing in their life savings to travel the country learning from people. I share this book in the hope that my interviews can serve you in the same way they served me: by helping find what was missing.

The experiences in this book changed my life. Let them change yours. Read the stories. Hear the quotes. And apply the wisdom to your own road.

CHAPTER ONE

A Seeker Goes On the Road
Andrew Harrison, Seeker

My journey began to take shape one February day that was a culmination of a battle that had been raging inside of me for years. I was 28 years old and living in Charlotte, North Carolina. At 10 a.m. my cell phone buzzed. The caller ID said it was my boss, Jeff Clark. I sold security guard contracts to businesses for Weiser Security Services, a company headquartered in New Orleans. He told me he was just about to get off of I-85 and onto 277. This put him five minutes away from my downtown apartment, 421 N. Graham St. #2A. My heart beat faster. I asked myself repeatedly, "Are you sure about this?"

The moment of truth did not wait for me to be ready. Jeff's blue Honda Civic with the LSU plates turned into the parking lot. I rocked back and forth nervously. Staring out the window of my apartment, I wasn't looking up at the crisp blue sky or the recently built skyline with the Bank of America and Wachovia buildings as I had so many times before. I was staring down and to my right, at Jeff, as he slowly made his way up the sidewalk toward my apartment. We had a golf outing that day, so he wasn't wearing our usual work attire of suit and tie. I had asked him to come to my apartment early, but didn't say why. My palms were sweating. He disappeared from my line of sight and I heard the familiar creak of the security gate after he entered the code. As he walked up the flight of stairs to the second floor, his steps echoed.

The sound of his steps grew louder as he approached my door. I took a few deep breaths—he'd be knocking momentarily. Months and months of questioning, thinking and planning had led up to this moment. "Hey Jeff," I said as I opened the door. We shook hands. Jeff was ten years older than me and he spoke with a New Orleans drawl. He stood about five-ten. Even though he talked about dieting a lot, he was thin. Shaggy hair flopped over his hazel eyes and he had a smile that was always sincere. Music was his thing and he was always making me CDs from bands such as the North Mississippi All Stars, Robert Randolph and the Family Band, and Galactic. He was a genuine guy and that was an asset in his sales and management style. Although Jeff was my boss, he was also my friend.

Because I had asked him to arrive early, Jeff walked in knowing something was up. After a handshake, small talk about traffic, golf and the weather, he asked, "So what's up, Bubba?"

"Well," I said and paused for a second. Many thoughts ran through my head. "Is this the right move? What will everyone say? Will he hate me? What about the money?" But I knew I had to tell him.

I breathed in, then quickly exhaled, "I've decided I'm resigning from Weiser." He didn't say anything. The look on his face painted a picture of a guy who got hit too hard in the stomach. I went on to say, "I'm not going to work for a competitor or taking another sales job. I'm not going to another job. I'm just not fired up by doing this anymore and it's not fair for me or for you guys. I need to see what else is out there."

He stared back at me. "What do you mean?"

"I'm just not motivated. I'm not putting in 100 percent effort and my attention to detail is proving it. That's not fair to you or to me." Actually voicing what I had thought about for so long was causing me to fumble my explanation.

He was still not sure how to react. He was not one to raise his voice, and he didn't. He gazed out the window, up at the skyline and said in wonder, "What are you talking about?"

"Jeff, this is a great job and I like working for you, but I'm just not passionate about it anymore. I need to see what else is out there, to see what other people are doing."

He asked again, his voice becoming more animated, "What do you mean, 'What else is out there?' What are you going to do if you're not going to work for anyone?"

If the look on his face was wonder, you should have seen the confusion after I explained, "I need to find the right career for me. I'm going to travel the country and interview people who are excited by their work." He stared at me and shook his head.

And then he gave me the look that had become all too familiar. When I told my friends what I was thinking of doing, they gave me "the look." When I told each of my different family members what I was thinking of doing, there it was. They all looked at me like I was speaking a foreign language.

Our conversation lasted about thirty minutes at the apartment and then another thirty in the car on the way to the golf course. I did my best to explain my lack of fulfillment and how I thought I would find it— through interviewing others.

It was obvious I could not try 100 jobs and see which one I liked best. My sales career had lasted four years. I knew I didn't have 400 years to figure this out. I reasoned that I could learn about 100 people's different careers by sitting down and interviewing them.

Jeff asked, "Are there that many people who love what they do?"

We both got a chuckle when I replied, "Hey, there better be. I don't have much of a choice but to find them." I knew I had met people who loved their work and I'd seen some on television. I knew they were out there. How to meet them was the second part of the equation. Once I identified them, the plan was simply to call or email for an interview. I could also connect to happy workers through friends and relatives. Once we were talking, I would ask them:

- What do you do?
- How did you get here?
- Are you happy with where you are?
    - ◇ Why?
- What would you do differently?
- What advice would you have for me as I try and figure out my career?

I would later learn that those six questions would open my mind to the world I had imagined and longed for as I tossed and turned during my sleepless nights in Charlotte.

Jeff continually peppered me with questions. The one that kept recurring was, "Are you OK?" After I laughed and reassured him that I was, he drilled me in more detail. "What about more money? What about a promotion? Is it the operations?"

I had to reaffirm that those were not the things causing me to leave. It was my lack of passion. It was hitting the snooze. It was not dotting the i's and crossing the t's. It was half-assing it, yet still being successful. That was not acceptable to me.

Jeff and I were playing in different golf groups that day; as he got into his cart he asked, "Are you sure about this? Do you know how much money you're leaving on the table?" He didn't wait for an answer as he sped off to the first tee box.

Jeff was right about the money. I was on pace to hit $100,000 without putting in 40 hours a week to do it. There were sales people at Weiser making more than $300,000 a year. Weiser was a great company to work for and I had a great management group to work under. It was obvious that Jeff wanted me to stay. Part of me wished that all my questions would vanish and I would stay with the life I had created for myself; the "good life."

After golf, he again asked about my reasons for leaving and I re-explained. He shook his head, still not comprehending. He asked me not to tell anyone else at Weiser and to sleep on it. Even though I had thought through this decision for months, I was still nervous about the finality of it. I agreed to spend the night thinking some more.

That night I had the apartment to myself and my mind was flying all over the place. Jeff's words echoed along with the voices of so many others close to me, "Are you sure about this?"

I couldn't sleep. I paced my bedroom. I slid my leather chair in front of my closet mirror and stared at myself. My blue eyes lost their focus in clouds of thought. I went outside and sat on the balcony, staring up at the familiar Bank of America and Wachovia buildings. The footsteps and laughter of three girls walking on the sidewalk echoed below. I looked down the street to the Panthers' football stadium. "Are you ready to sacrifice all of this?" I said out loud. I paced, I sat, I moved to another spot and I paced some more.

My life would change incredibly if I went through with this. There would be no more golf trips, $200 dinner dates or new clothes. Establishing a relationship with a girlfriend potentially leading to marriage and kids would probably need to be put on hold. All that I had pictured and imagined for most of my life was about to be altered.

Moving back inside, I thought back on the previous few months. I was an unhappy person and I wondered what would change if I decided to stay. If I pressed on, I would surely make more money and I could buy some new "toys," which was always fun. I thought about finding a wife, settling down and buying a house. Charlotte was a place where I believed I could grow old. My pacing and sitting and standing and thinking turned into hours. Even though it was well past midnight I picked up my phone to get Jeff's advice but hung up before I hit send. "This is on you," I said again out loud.

I lay back down, but there was no REM in my future. I paced more, poured a glass of chocolate milk and sat at my desk, staring at the computer screen. An ominous silence shrouded my apartment. The only illumination in the room emanated from my laptop and the bright white of Microsoft Outlook. I locked my eyes on the screen, to the open email entitled, "Andrew Harrison: Resignation Letter." The "To:" section listed Jeff and the COO of our company.

My chair squeaked as I leaned back with my hands clasped behind my head. The reality was now hitting me. "Are you sure about this, Andrew?" I asked myself.

I still wasn't sure and got up again, walking back to the balcony. The lighted skyline stared down at me, but didn't offer any advice. I moved back inside to my desk.

Grabbing a sheet of paper from the printer I scribbled down some of the questions I had been asking myself. "Is this how work is supposed to feel? Am I making a difference? Will I feel like this for the next 30 years? Why am I here? What is my purpose? I have hit my goals, why aren't I happy? Everyone else wants what I have, why don't I? What is wrong with me?" The one I circled was, "What is my purpose?"

I flipped the page over. I am no mathematician, but I started jotting down numbers. Eventually, a Work Equation jumped off the page. If I work from age 23 to age 65, that is 42 years on the job. I ball parked 40 hours per week of work and 50 weeks per year.

Work Equation:

42 years of work X 40 hours per week X 50 weeks per year = 84,000 Hours at Work

The numbers gave me a Mike Tyson punch to my milk-filled belly. My thoughts of not being accepted and the fear of losing all of the things I had accumulated whooshed out of me. I stared at the equation. The numbers shocked me. After a long trance, I told myself, "If I have to spend 84,000 hours of my life working, I've got to be passionate about it."

I swiveled back to the computer and "84,000 Hours" was the only thing that pulsed in my head. The screen looked up at me. I re-read my resignation letter a few times. I got up and paced one more time. I then sat rigidly in my chair, close to the keyboard. Drawing a deep breath, I said, "Here we go." I clicked the mouse. The email was sent. My decision was final. I had expected an immediate phone call or email. There was only silence.

I had just quit the job everyone but me wanted.

Resigning was the climax of a 28-year battle that had been raging inside of me. I had always wanted to live by my own rules, but I had done what seemed "right." I had done what I was supposed to. I was always scared. I had been scared for so long that I had gone through life without knowing my value system. I was scared of not being accepted. Scared of not having money. Scared of angering parents or family members. Scared of what others thought. Scared of rejection. Scared of the boss. Scared of not using my education. Scared of the unknown. Scared of crime. Scared of loneliness. Scared of injury. Scared of failure. As good as I had it, my resignation day was the first time I truly felt like I was actually living my own life.

It's funny, though I was still so unclear on what I wanted to do for my career, I was entirely sure that the journey would provide my answers. I don't know where the confidence came from, but my inner voice kept telling me to go for it—that I would regret it if I didn't. I didn't care that my friends didn't get it. I didn't care that I was giving up more money than I had ever made. Most people, once they heard, asked me if I was okay. I didn't care. There was an inner peace about me as I pummeled the fear that had won so many battles for so many years of my life.

With as much positive energy as I had, there was still trepidation about money. My budget was limited and if I wanted to make the full circle, I was going to have to make some major changes in my spending habits. Expensive meals, bar tabs and golf courses were for special occasions. Hotels were looked at as a last resort. Shopping for new clothes was taboo. I'd have to make do with what I had. I said goodbye to my nice things and focused on my new priorities: car payment, gas and medical insurance.

The people at Weiser did not understand my decision. They sent me to an industrial psychologist. They offered me more money. They offered to fly me to Florida to talk with their most tenured salesperson over rounds of golf. They talked about a change in the operations. They talked about giving me more creativity in my work. It was too late. As I told Jeff at my apartment, I had to find my purpose.

My friends still didn't fully understand, but they were supportive. As for my parents, they were obviously confused. My dad had a one-company career, retiring from Kodak after 42 years. My mom stayed at home with the hardest job there is: taking care of the kids (my younger sister and me). After a lot of hesitation and heart-to heart-talks, my parents were behind me. But the most important person was now on board full throttle—me. I had not felt self-confidence in a long time and I now had it in abundance. I spent the weeks leading up to my last day of work transitioning my sales accounts to Jeff and starting to conduct interviews locally in Charlotte. The stories of people who liked their job helped calm my fears.

I also had to prepare for going on the road. This meant securing a 10 x 10 storage unit for my furnishings, changing the addresses on my personal accounts to my parents' address in western New York and getting checked out by my doctors during my final days under company-paid health insurance. While still showing an income, I switched cars, trading in my 2001 four-door sedan for a new 2004 SUV so that, if necessary, I could sleep in my vehicle as I traveled.

My mind zeroed in on the journey. As a salesperson, I knew that in order for me to get interviews with people, I couldn't be looked at as a hippie or weirdo. They had to see me as a guy on a life mission. Doug Wood, one of my friends from grad school at the University of South Carolina, created the graphics template for my website, www.iamontheroad.com.

I found Bobby Blake, a 20-year-old Kappa Sigma fraternity brother from my alma mater, the University of Arkansas at Little Rock, to build the inside and databases of the website.

The website would give me credibility and help out with all of the family and friends who would otherwise be calling me to see where I was and if I was okay. I didn't want to be on the phone all of the time; I wanted to be living the journey. Bobby included a Journal link on the site that I could update wherever I had a web connection.

My sales background also showed me the importance of business cards in face-to-face meetings. I might have left my job, but I was still a business man. I had cards made up with my name, website, phone number and e-fax number. When I called the print shop, they took down that information and asked me for my title. I told them I had no idea and I'd call them back.

"What is my title?" I wondered. I wasn't starting a company so I wasn't the owner or CEO of anything. I wasn't a consultant as my Weiser cards read. I went to Dictionary.com and entered some words but nothing resonated. Then a word popped into my head. I looked it up and the entry made my eyes pop:

"Seeker: someone making a search or inquiry; one that seeks: *a seeker of the truth.*"

I called the print shop back and a Seeker I became.

The Weiser executives did what they could to keep me at arms' reach for, as they said, "When I'd snap out of it." They kept my job open with the idea that I would come back when this was out of my system. I agreed to do some contract marketing work for them as I traveled and this paid me between $600 and $900 a month, depending on what I did. The money would obviously help along the way. My budget was tight. I had around $6,000 in my savings account and another $2,000 in my checking to take me as far as I could go. My entourage was my SUV stuffed to the gills with a new Canon video camera with passenger seat mount, a refurbished Sony mini cassette tape recorder, a Kodak Easy Share digital camera, some notebooks I would use as journals, my Weiser Compaq Evo laptop, my cell phone, golf clubs, tent, sleeping bag, clothes for all seasons, laundry detergent, CD collection and credit and debit cards.

Two months prior to my twenty-ninth birthday, I said goodbye to my family, my friends and my city, setting out for a life journey into the unknown. I was on the road!

What unfolded over 75,000 miles and 145 interviews changed my life, my values and me, forever. My interview experiences were not about titles, salaries or specific jobs. They were about the energy and feelings each person has because of their job. As I sat across from each interviewee, their passion intoxicated and filled me. Their experiences and advice caused a metamorphosis in me. I went from scared and uninspired to brave and amped up beyond belief.

It is now my job to pay forward their passion to you. The following 11 lessons and 33 interview chapters will connect you to my inspiring friends and help you to navigate your own career and life road. Your time is now! Hop into my passenger seat, buckle up and join me on an amazing journey for a life of purpose and passion.

LESSON ONE

Debunking the Work Myth

The preconceived notion many of us share is that no one loves their job. I bought into this Work Myth for much of my career. When I was done with college, there was no job or field that I felt called to enter. I didn't have a true passion for anything. So I listened to the Work Myth. No one loves their job, so it doesn't matter if I do.

Based on this assumption, my career goal was to make as much money as I could while working the least amount of hours to make it. I realize this was not noble, but it was my goal. I went into the sales field, and after four years, I excelled at my dream job.

I was on my way to $100,000 a year (and more). I rarely worked more than 40 hours per week. I worked from home and set my own schedule. I could sleep in, go golfing, go to the gym and travel. So, I did.

Yet, even though I had my dream job of money, time and freedom, I wasn't happy. And I started to wonder if everyone felt as uninspired by their work as I did. I would voice my dissatisfaction to my friends and many of them would tell me, "C'mon Andrew, what are you talking about? You have it so much better than I do." And they would proceed to list why my job was better than theirs. And they were right. But it still didn't make me feel good.

Some days I would tell myself, "Okay, this is the week. We are going to get fired up about work." That positive energy was fleeting. On other days I would tell myself, "Hey idiot, take a look around. You have it great. Quit complaining and get to work." This would help for short bursts.

As I would toss and turn at night wondering what was wrong with me, I repeated the many reasons why I should just suck it up and live the "good life." The main thing I came back to was that no one loves what they do; therefore I should just plod along with my lack of passion. That I should be happy to have a nice paycheck and a nice place to live. That no one is fired up by their work, so I should just fall in line.

Yet, as I plodded around in my confused state, I began to watch and to listen. I tried to see if there were in fact people who loved what they did. With a new set of eyes and ears; I read books, magazines and newspapers. I watched TV, I listened to the radio and I analyzed my interactions with people.

Only when I was looking for it did I see and appreciate that there were people who loved what they did. They were always there, but the Work Myth blinded me. It's like one of those paintings that you have to stare at for a while to see what is in it. If you don't concentrate, it is a blobby blur. You don't see anything. Yet, if you focus, you can see a lot of things.

I didn't have to search hard to find what I was looking for: people who were filled with purpose and passion by their work. That is when I decided that I had to go on the road and get to know these people. That I had to interview them to find out how they got to where they were and what their advice would be for me.

I met them in some expected professions: teacher, doctor, police officer, medical researcher, small business owner and firefighter. Others surprised me: Financial planner, secretary, maintenance man, strip club manager, branding expert, newspaper columnist and publicist.

The people I met tossed my Work Myth to the curb. Once I saw and believed that there truly were people who love their job and life, I knew I had to become one of them. I did become one of them. I am one of them. And my goal is for you to become one of them.

That is exactly what Lesson One is about. The Work Myth is bunk. Yes, there are a lot of people who hate their job. But, once you believe that there are people who love their work, then you can get on the road to becoming one of them.

This entire book is filled with accounts of people working and living with purpose and passion, but the next two chapters showcase people who undeniably typify the inspired life.

CHAPTER TWO

No Doubt About It
A life and death perspective

You may think you love a job, but until you are presented with death, you don't know what your priorities will be. In my case, I knock on wood when I say that I haven't had to encounter my own personal questions of mortality. In the case of Fred Story, his diverse career in music has played out to answer a question many of us wonder about: "If you knew you had only so long to live, what would you do for the rest of your time?"

Our interview took place in Charlotte, North Carolina, not far from the Carolina Panthers' football stadium, at Fred's studio, Concentrix Music and Sound Design. The lobby of Concentrix was decorated with pictures and awards, the clutter of a successful music studio. Fred came into the dimly lit room. He stood around six-two and wore jeans, a black shirt and sandals. As he approached, he limped.

We walked around the different studios and offices and Fred introduced me to his employees and his wife, Becky. Everyone was working hard and barely looked up to acknowledge me.

We made our way into Fred's space, a combination of studio and office. The computer monitors, mixing boards and dozens of switches and knobs made the office resemble a cockpit.

"You might say we are all pre-wired to do certain things," Fred began. He grew up surrounded by music, just like his father before him. One of Fred's uncles played with well-known blues musicians, Flatt and Scruggs as well as with the Louvin brothers. His father was in the Air Force, so they moved often during his elementary school years. But wherever they went, his father had a band. His son soon followed his musical footsteps.

"I grew up around country music and from the time I was old enough to pick up something, I could play it." As a child, Fred could play the theme songs from Bonanza and Captain Kangaroo on his grandmother's piano even though he could barely reach the keys. Formal music training began in middle school, when he joined band. "Music was always the thing for me. The mold was cast."

The trombone and piano were Fred's first instruments and he learned to read music for the first time in seventh grade while being mentored by his band director. At that point, he told me his goal was to teach music or be a high school band director himself. The goal carried him to college at East Tennessee State University where he majored in music.

At school, a side job in radio changed the course of Fred's career plans. He had been working in radio during high school and picked up another gig in college. In his deep, clear voice, a voice that would boom out from the radio, he explained: "Radio is a fun thing when you're young. In college I was working for the #1 top 40 station in town and had a little showbiz factor. I had friends who were getting out and teaching full time as band directors, but I was working part time in radio and making more money than they were. I got enamored with it and took my eye off the prize, the band director job."

We talked briefly about how more money or an ego boost can sometimes shift our focus. In many cases, the focus comes back. That's what happened to Fred.

After a few years, he learned being on the air was fun, but not what he truly enjoyed; it was the production, the commercials and doing the off-the-air stuff that energized him. He moved behind the scenes as a production director.

Even though he made his money in radio production, Fred never lost his passion for playing and writing music. He admits his writing was better than his playing. "Writing was always my first love. I would reserve a practice room for two hours. I'd go in and tell myself 'You have two hours to practice, so practice.'" He hummed some musical notes to himself and played an imaginary piano. In a higher pitched voice, as if his brain was speaking to himself, "Oh, I hear a melody. How can I harmonize that?" He shook his head and grinned. "At the end of two hours, I'd written a tune but I hadn't practiced a lick. So I was always a lame player."

In 1981, Fred was in his mid-twenties and moved to Charlotte. He was working behind the scenes at a rock station and formed a band with two guys. The band, under the names Fly One Away and Flight 108, produced four albums over 13 years. Touring the Southeast to play festivals, Fly One Away opened for the likes of Ray Charles, Kenny G, Dave Sanborn and Earl Clue.

"It was the most fun I've ever had playing music. People got to know our tunes and request our tunes. Once the band got out there, I got known as a guy who could write tunes." Playing with the band soon led to another career opportunity.

"Out of the blue I got a call to write a jingle for a Belk ad (a department store chain in the southeast)." He enjoyed writing the jingle. Another agency heard his work and two weeks later he got another jingle request. Fred was now known in the advertising world.

The combination of enjoying writing jingles and the paychecks they brought convinced Fred that, while radio and touring was fine, a studio and writing music might be something he'd want to do down the road full time. "It's really fun and it's a way you can make a living doing music without having to travel and deal with all of the lifestyle garbage," he explained.

The true turning point in Fred's career had nothing to do with him. It had everything to do with a teacher. Fred's initial goal in studying with a teacher was to try to hone his piano skills for the band. But in their first 15 minutes together, his teacher, Ziggy Hurwitz, saw something else in Fred. "Everything that's important I learned from Ziggy. He's the reason I'm doing this."

Fred paused, and his expression grew serious. "Ziggy changed my life. It is the closest thing I'll ever experience to the European tradition of the teacher and the student, the mentor."

Fred explained, "He really took me aback. Ziggy said, 'If you want to learn how to play better, I don't think I can help you with that. But I don't think that's what you really want to do.' I told him composing is my first love, writing music is what I love to do and is what always gives me the most satisfaction. Ziggy said, 'Ahh. That I can help you with.' And I studied under him for seven years."

To write and compose music the way he wanted, Fred decided to open his own studio. He and his second wife, Becky, made a pact, taking all the money he made from doing the new jingle work and sinking it into trying to build a studio one piece at a time. "At some point I realized this was not something I may do, this was something I had to do."

All of the experiences Fred had up to that point were necessary for his success. Twenty years of production prepared him to open his own studio. "I had a great training ground, especially the production skills.

"Some people come back to stuff late in life and figure it out. I'll be 49 next month. Any day I can write music is a good day."

As I listened to Fred, it was amazing. Here was a guy whose passion for music had always been a part of his life. But even with that, his road had taken numerous forks within the music industry. It took all of his experiences and Ziggy to bring out Fred's true passion: writing music.

Fred told me he often gets calls from people wanting to get into the music industry. His advice can be applied to most passions. "What you need to do first is decide what role music must play in your life. There are lots of ways for music to be in your life that don't require it to be your profession, or to have music as a profession without being a star."

The chance to live his advice presented itself a few years prior to our meeting. Fred had started scoring movies and because he was good, was asked to do some big independent films. But to get to the big time of feature films, you have to be in Hollywood.

He and Becky deliberated for a long time on whether or not they should make the move to L.A. "Will I be happy if I never get to score a major Hollywood feature? Will I die unfulfilled if I never get to do that?" he asked out loud.

He suddenly swiveled in his chair, and played a NAPA Auto Parts commercial he was working on. He had me listen to the range of the music. "See, it's just like a car whirring by."

Fred swung his chair back around, "We really labored over L.A. Do we go for the brass ring?" he said and set a steady gaze on me. "You've got to find your own brass ring.

"So many satisfying things have happened. The work. The crew here. None of that would have happened if I had hauled my ass to L.A.," he said.

Then Fred went back to the influence of Ziggy. "The most pretentious thing I could say is that I could ever be a Ziggy to someone. If I could just give a fraction of it back—when someone is such an influence in your life, it creates this natural desire to make sure that the lessons don't stop with you."

For his employees, Fred hopes he will be the type of mentor that Ziggy was for him. "I guess I'm a different kind of band leader now."

I thought the interview was going to end there. I almost leaned in to turn off the cassette tape, but Fred stared me down, like he was sizing me up. I must have passed because he said Hollywood had tempted him, but his decision to stay in Charlotte was validated by a brush with mortality. Four years prior to our interview, Fred started having health problems that his doctors eventually diagnosed as Lou Gehrig's disease. That's where his limp came from. Faced with the threat of losing control of his body, and eventually his life, to the crippling disease, Fred did some intense soul-searching.

"The first thing I told Becky was 'Well, they tell me I only have a couple of years to live,'" he said and paused. "It's funny; a parting question is always theoretical: 'So if you knew you had only so long to live what would you do for the rest of your time?'

"In my case, this certainly wasn't theoretical. I told Becky I don't want to climb Mount Everest or sail around the world. I didn't want to do that when I was healthy, why would I want to do that now? All I remember thinking the whole time is that I have got to write as much music as I can. I've got to write as much music as I can. I've got to write as much music as I can.

"What more affirmation can you get that you're doing the thing you ought to be doing? What few thoughts I might have had going into this—as far as, 'Am I doing what I'm supposed to be doing?'—you know what? They are asked and answered for the rest of my life. I'll never have to ask that question again. I don't think there is any way that I could ever be more certain. I'll change and the job will change and the finances will change, but as far as am I doing what I'm supposed to be doing? There is absolutely zero doubt."

• • • • • • • • • • • • • • • • • •

REWIND

- Since he was a boy, Fred knew music was his passion. Yet, the role music played in his career evolved over time. He wanted to be a band director, then was a radio personality, did production behind the scenes, toured as a musician and then started his own business as a composer. The titles changed, but the core of it all, the music, did not. Fred showed me that if we have a talent and a passion for something specific, we shouldn't pigeonhole ourselves. We can apply that passion to many different jobs.

- Fred's experiences are the initial interview chapter because he shows beyond a shadow of a doubt—there are people who love what they do. When he was diagnosed with Lou Gehrig's disease, Fred's passion for music didn't go away; it grew even stronger. Fred didn't want to take a vacation; he wanted to go to work and make as much music as he could.

  I don't want to be faced with Fred's question, "If you knew you had only so long to live, what would you do for the rest of your time?" But if I were, I would want my answer to be the same — "live my passion for as long as I can."

Important side note: As it turned out, Fred's condition was not Lou Gehrig's disease, but an even more rare disorder known as Myasthenia Gravis, a neuromuscular disorder that weakens voluntary muscles. By taking three pills a day, Fred can't push it, but he is able to function almost normally. Even more importantly, this disease is rarely fatal.

CHAPTER THREE

The Ideal Situation
My job is who I am

In Hollywood, Florida, I interviewed a woman who epitomizes love for her job. Teresita "Terri" Wardlow's journey to her passionate work as a high school guidance counselor did not come easily. After some bends and forks, her ideal road became clear. She's had her foot on the gas ever since.

As a little girl, Terri's dream was to become a teacher. "I remember vividly sitting my sister down, who is five years younger than me, and pretending I was the teacher and teaching her using the blackboard my mother bought me."

She always loved math, but in college she detoured from the teaching dream in order to study computer programming. In school, someone asked her, 'Why don't you become a teacher?' She quickly brushed that aside. "I said 'No way, they make no money.' That was probably the biggest mistake I ever made."

Terri's experience of shunning her dream because of perceived money issues is quite common. We may have an inclination of what our passion is but we devalue our path and allow ourselves to be influenced by outside factors: the money or social status attributed to our dream job as opposed to another job we can acquire, or other people's opinions or societal stereotypes.

Once Terri graduated, she found work in the computer industry. After a few months on the job, she began to question her career choices. "I was in an office sitting in front of a computer all day and was so unhappy. I was absolutely miserable. I hated it. I figured what I missed was people."

Because she hated the work, Terri found it impossible to give it her best effort. That compounded her frustration, so she left, going to an

Terri, her husband, Joey, and their son JJ.

accounting job for a company that sold radio commercials. "It was better, but I still wasn't happy. At least my salary was covering my bills."

Still largely dissatisfied with work, Terri sought an outlet to address her 'people and passion' needs. She found herself getting involved with the young adult group in her church. The passion missing in her nine-to-five life was soon found in working with kids. A fire was lit. "I loved it. I just loved it."

It turned out that a lot of her co-workers at the church were teachers. After a period of self-reflection, Terri began querying her co-workers about their work and whether they thought she might make a good teacher. It was clear they thought she was a natural.

After more analysis, Terri made the leap back onto her dream path. She applied and was accepted as a teacher of religion at Monsignor Pace, a private catholic school in Fort Lauderdale.

Her Cuban heritage was an ideal fit for the predominantly Hispanic school. "I related to the kids so well. I grew up with the same rules and regulations as in their households. I understood them."

The diocese's rule was that if you had a bachelor's degree you could teach as long as you took classes towards getting your education certificate. Terri had to go back to school. "As soon as I walked into my first class I felt like a sponge. I had never felt like that before. I couldn't get enough information."

That positive energy never left. Terri excelled at school and in her teaching. Terri's newfound passion allowed her to take on tasks and responsibilities usually reserved for more senior people. In her third year as a teacher, she became the department head. Soon after, she was offered the role of the campus minister at the school. "I did so much in a five year span, I can't remember it all," she laughed.

At this point in her story, Terri's eyes got big and her ear-to-ear smile filled the room. "I look at teaching not as a job but as my vocation. It's who I am. It's what I do. That's the only way I can explain it."

This quote from Terri has stayed with me ever since. I use it in my own life and in the talks that I give. My career goal is to get everyone to see their job not just as a job, but as their vocation, as who they are.

When Terri took some classes for additional certification and met Dr. Adriana McEachern, they clicked immediately. "I guess she saw something in me. She inspired me to do more. She became my mentor." Terri's love of personal interaction with her kids and Dr. McEachern's influence led to a slight shift in Terri's career focus. After 13 years of teaching, Terri went for a Masters in Guidance.

Terri was once again a sponge. The minimum number of credits required for graduation was 30; she graduated with 60 credits.

Passion continued to propel Terri to additional success. At the time of our interview, she was the guidance director at Monsignor Pace and the first private school counselor to become the vice president of the Florida Counseling Association. She was also in her third year as an adjunct professor at St. Thomas University teaching legal and ethical issues for a graduate program in counseling. "If I like what I do, I can do a lot."

As a counselor, Terri tries to help others avoid some of the pitfalls she experienced during her education and career evolution. "I love the psychology of it, the analyzing and figuring out." She starts by asking basic questions and trying to fit the student's interests and skills to college or job choices. She asks, "What do you like? What intrigues you? What catches your attention?" Then she expands on the answers.

"It could be as simple as, 'I doodle a lot.' That means you like to draw. 'But I like math, too.' If you like to draw and you like math, maybe architecture. All that I am asking them is, 'What do you like to do?' And then we look at it.

"It's a matter of finding what you like, then taking what you like and creating whatever it is. 'What are you good at?' is my next question. I tell the kids that you might like to sing, but you can't sing a note, so we need to be realistic. Some say 'I just doodle,' and they'll show me an art piece that is amazing. Sweetheart, look at what you can do. 'But I just do that.' Did you ever consider this was your God-given gift? So why don't you enhance that gift because you don't need to think twice about it."

Then, Terri's voice became measured. "We have to combat the same thing I faced when I was their age: the money issue. They say they want to be a lawyer so they can make all this money, but we see their personality doesn't fit that career. Some of the kids think of money first and we try to get them to think about other things. It's not about the money; it's about the love for what you are doing. Trust me, it's not about the money," she laughed.

Next, Terri started talking about the students and alumni she bumps into outside of work. "I love the fact they are so excited to see me."

She taught Alex Fernandez, who is a Major League Baseball player. Another student, Tony Egues became the youngest equipment manager in the history of the NFL for the Miami Dolphins and was a consultant for the movie *Any Given Sunday*. She also talked fondly of kids who didn't turn out as prominently, including a student who came to see her after getting out of rehab and another who came to see her a few days a week before going to jail.

"I'm just as happy to have taught them as I am Alex and Tony. Sometimes even more so because I know the struggle and the learning experiences they've had. When I see these kids and they thank me for my work, it makes me feel good that I impacted their lives somehow. To think that I planted this tiny seed and it grew is wonderful," she said with a gleam in her eye.

"I remember my first couple of years on the job, there was a teacher who was so burned out and mean. She was so negative to the kids and to her co-workers. I remember looking at her and saying, 'If I ever hate what

I do that much, I will quit.' I cannot imagine getting up each morning and hating that I have to go somewhere. I just can't. And the moment I do, I'll quit. I couldn't care less about the money. Are there times I'm exhausted? Oh yes. Have I been stressed to the max? Yes. But it never deters me."

Terri sighed and smiled. "All of that I guess is why I do what I do. I don't know, I just know it has become who I am."

REWIND

- Terri showed me how transformational passion can be. She initially shied away from teaching because of money perceptions. Later, she went from looking for an outlet away from a job she didn't like to working at a teaching job she loved. And when her passion was there, dedicated effort followed.

  When your talents and passions are aligned, you will take 60 credits when you only need 30. You will stay past five o'clock. Your work won't always feel like work. You will be recognized as a leader. You will make an impact on those around you.

- I can only imagine how much better our world would be if everyone could share Terri's feelings about work, "I look at this not as a job but as my vocation. It's who I am. It's what I do." The Ripple Effect would be incredibly positive...

LESSON TWO

The Ripple Effect

Fred Story and Terri Wardlow just showed us that there are people who love their job. We also saw how their passion had a Ripple Effect in the way they influenced the people they came into contact with. This next lesson shows that it truly matters if you love what you do. As I have experienced from my interviewees and in my own journey; there is a Ripple Effect. Your work life carries over to your community and home life.

If 84,000 hours of our life will be spent at work, and we dread what we are doing, it is hard to be happy when we are not at work. At the same time, if we love what we do for our 84,000 hours, it makes being happy with our life so much easier.

When I give talks at colleges, I have the students raise their hands and answer, "How many of your parents like their job?" A few hands go up. Then I ask, "How many of your parents hate their job?" The number of raised hands skyrocket. Whether it's positive or negative, I know kids feel the Ripple Effect of their parents.

Human nature dictates that when we don't like doing something, we let it rub off on others. We tell people about it. We complain about the boss, or the company, or the work, or the pay, or our co-workers. We get the Sunday Night Blues. We also don't work as hard as we could. We become de-motivated. We become a "clock watcher," doing just enough to keep our job. This has an impact on everyone we work with.

Yet, human nature strives to succeed. Babies are not born with the desire to screw up. It does not feel good to fail. We don't get excited about how "actively disengaged" we are. Inside, it does not feel good to be a clock watcher.

We want to put effort into our work. We want to be excited. We want to be passionate. Yet, past stats show that the United States is not in a great place with regard to work.

CareerBuilder did a study which states that less than 50 percent of people look forward to going to work.

Gallup says that only 29 percent of people are "engaged" by their work, explaining, "Engaged employees work with passion and feel a profound connection to their company. They drive innovation and move the organization forward."

Gallup also says, "Actively disengaged employees cost U.S. companies $254 to $363 billion annually."

So, if we have to spend 84,000 hours of life at work, and half of us don't look forward to going to work, and only 29 percent are engaged by what we do, what does that mean? To me, it means work sucks for a lot of people. And when we feel like our work sucks, we look for an escape.

As an example, when Terri Wardlow hated her accounting job, she looked to things outside of work to lift her up. She became involved with the young adult group at her church. And this eventually led her to the teaching field. How wonderful for Terri (and the kids she worked with). Her escape was very positive.

When I didn't like my job, I also looked to escape. I regret to say, I wasn't spending time with the youth group.

On the "good" side: I went to the gym, watched movies, attended church, read books, cooked dinners, dated women, traveled, spent time with family and friends, golfed and played basketball.

On the "not-so-good" side: I wasted a ton of money, was not forthcoming with the women I dated and partied my butt off. These admissions may not allow me to run for President of the United States (or they may help get me elected), but I put them out here to let you know that some people walk a fine line with their escapism. I've lost five percent of my body weight in a 24-hour span due to alcohol poisoning. I've driven a car when I shouldn't have. I've lost friends due to drunken phone calls. I've had some ravenous cases of the munchies. And I've seen what my face looks like inching closer and closer to a mirror that is lying flat on a table.

I have lived the negative Ripple Effect. I have experienced firsthand what happens when we do not like what we do for work. We look to things outside of work to provide us fulfillment. And, we don't know the impact of the ripple. Sometimes we find positive things. Sometimes we find negative things.

I want you to see that escapism has real-life consequences. Alcohol and drug abuse, divorce and family arguments can stem from work-related issues.

Remember what Terri Wardlow said about her job? "I look at teaching not as a job but as my vocation. It's who I am. It's what I do." Fred Story was told he had a terminal disease and resolved to make as much music as he could. I often imagine what our families, what our society, and what our world would be like if everyone had the same feelings as Terri and Fred do about their jobs. The Ripple Effect would be an incredible power for good.

To recap, if you love your job, the Ripple Effect on you and the people around you will more than likely be positive. If you detest your job, it will be hard to avoid a negative Ripple Effect.

The two chapters which follow will introduce you to people who have battled through the negative Ripple Effect with some interesting results.

CHAPTER FOUR

When the Childhood Dream Doesn't Go Away
Choosing between $100,000 or $14,000 a year

Some people are fortunate enough to be working at their childhood dream job. Other people still carry their childhood vision, but haven't pursued it. They've ended up with a different education and work in a different field. The question they may ask is, "What if the thing I wanted to do as a child is still with me?"

Geoff Calkins is someone who has answered this question. Our talk took place as we drove to and from his sports talk radio show in Memphis, Tennessee. He walked out of his brick house on the upper-middle-class east side of Memphis wearing shorts, loafers with no socks and an un-tucked blue golf shirt buttoned once. We decided to take his car, an older, light blue minivan, which was strewn with empty Coke cans and crumpled up papers.

"If you asked me what I wanted to be when I was 12, I would've said to be that guy in the newspaper who gets to tell people what he thinks about sports and have his picture next to the column," he said as he turned the wheel and merged with traffic. "But, at some point I started thinking, 'That's unrealistic. It's like wanting to grow up to be a cowboy; people don't really do that.'"

We all have put family pressure on ourselves, but Geoff must have really felt it. He comes from a stellar, high-achieving group of relatives. Both of his parents were doctors with strong work ethics. He is one of nine kids and all of his five brothers attended Harvard University for college or graduate school.

He was brought up surrounded by success as well as support. "We learned from my father that your work is supposed to be something more than financial, it is supposed to be your pleasure and your passion.

He's 82 and still works. My mom just retired; she's about to turn 80. The main thing was not money or prestige. My dad, for example, never had a car costing more than $10,000. He was a used car guy," Geoff said as he slowed his own used car for a red light.

As he went over his family background, I expected him to tell me he was the rebel, the one brother who didn't go to Harvard; but that was not the case. The sports columnist at the *Memphis Commercial Appeal* was a Harvard educated lawyer.

As a 12-year-old boy, Geoff hadn't thought that his dream was attainable or sustainable. Yet, he still worked at his high school paper, but ended up entering Harvard in pre-law. There, working for Harvard's school paper, he still satisfied his taste for journalism. Although he excelled at his pre-law classes, he thought enough about journalism to work one summer for *People* magazine and another at the *Miami Herald*. He was even offered a non-sports writing job at a newspaper in Fort Myers, Florida. "If I was going to be a writer, I had to be a sportswriter. And yet, because I went to Harvard, I sort of thought I should take myself more seriously than sports writing."

After Harvard it was decision time. He applied to both journalism school and law school, but still carried the feeling that becoming a sports columnist was a pipe dream. He did some soul searching at that point, going on a fellowship to Australia. "I thought that by sitting over there and taking a year off, I could figure out what I wanted to do. I learned drinking beer and looking at your big toe contemplating the universe is not how you figure out what you want do," he said as we laughed.

"I think you figure out what you want to do by doing different things. Try something and decide if you like it. When you have experiences, something might catch your interest or surprise you. All you can do is go at it with everything you have and see where it takes you."

Up until he decided to go to Australia, Geoff had made all of the "right" choices. He got As in high school. He went to Harvard. He got As there. The next "right" decision was made when he chose Harvard Law School, not journalism school. He also got As there. Geoff was smart. He graduated magna cum laude from both Harvard University and Harvard Law School.

"There was never pressure from my family to be a lawyer. In fact everyone who knows me said that I should not become a lawyer. I'm disorganized, laid back, happy-go-lucky. And I lose things." As he spoke, I gazed down at the cans and papers on the floor of the car.

He paused at this point, took his eyes off the stopped traffic and focused on me, "The moment I set foot in my first legal methods class at Harvard Law School, I knew that it was not for me. I got this grinding feeling in my stomach. 'Oh my gosh, this is not right.' All along I was thinking, 'How am I going to hit the eject button here?' I used to think about trying to get a joint degree. But I kept going."

As law school progressed, it still didn't feel right, but he pushed on despite his misgivings. He graduated and clerked for a year at the US Court of Appeals in Washington, DC. Then Geoff joined a law firm to see if it would light his fire.

Working for the firm brought him success and money. Yet, as he rocketed his way upward, his need for inspiration grew. "I didn't want to be that guy in the corner office. I disliked every single bit of it. I had to gut myself to do it every day. I was truly struggling. It was an act of will."

Geoff had battled for years with not having passion for his schooling and his work. Yet, he still excelled at what he did. "But at some point, it became more than just this nagging feeling that it wasn't right. It became a full-scale depression. I just didn't like my work. I was 28 and asked myself, 'How could it have possibly worked out like this? I did everything right.'"

His attraction to journalism still persisted. Although it had been eight years since he had formally written anything and his law career was on the rise; he applied to Columbia School of Journalism and was accepted. After some deliberation, he went for it, taking a leave of absence from the law firm. The leave status allowed him to return if things didn't work out with journalism.

Geoff excelled at Columbia just as he had at Harvard. He had recently become engaged, and upon graduation it was time to go to work. He wrote to 300 newspapers applying for a job, but his letters elicited little response. Discouraged, he was in talks to go back to the law firm. They were offering him close to $100,000. Then he got a call from the *Anniston Star* in Anniston, Alabama. He had never been to Anniston. They offered him a 12-week internship covering high school sports, paying around $225 a week.

Now married, Geoff was at another fork in the road. He had a spouse to think about as part of this choice. "It was a major decision, but we took the newspaper job and went to Anniston," he said turning the wheel squeezing into moving traffic. We discussed how he finally decided to go for it. Geoff talked about moments of self-recognition. "I finally understood myself.

"I loved it from day one," Geoff responded as he smiled. "It wasn't all roses. I'm in Anniston, Julie and I were newly married and I'm making like 14 grand. There were stages there where I said, 'OK, even though I want to do this and love it...'" and he cut himself off. "It clicked instantly. I really loved it."

Geoff's family embraced his new career. "In the end, they just wanted me to be happy."

Geoff's story gets him calls from people who are not happy with their job and want to become sports columnists. As he told me his standard response, I could sense stress in his voice. The tone was slow and thought-out: "It is such a hard business. You have to be willing to go anywhere and to write anything. I moved to Anniston, Alabama for $225 a week and wrote about high school sports. I still got so lucky along the way and I got so many breaks." He shook his head.

Geoff had shot up the journalism ranks, a rise that is not at all typical. He went from being a prep writer in Anniston to the columnist in Memphis in four years. "In this city there are probably 800 successful, happy lawyers. There is only one newspaper and we have eight writers in our sports department. There is only one job in this whole city that I ultimately would want as a sports writer and I have it," he said as he again shook his head.

His voice was now more upbeat. "I've got to tell you, I'm torn on the advice. I can't imagine my life if I had not made the switch. I think it would have ended very unhappily. I cannot imagine it. I can't think of anything else I would have really done and done well. I can't possibly conceive my life without making the change I made."

I asked him if he would do anything differently. "You have to look at the failed experiences as positive ones, too. I now know I am not supposed to be a lawyer. One of the great things about our society and our economy is that lots of people are switching jobs all the time. I think you can have two or three careers and you can remake yourself."

One of the reasons people gave him for being unhappy with their jobs was their perceived lack of impact on society. I asked whether there was more impact being a lawyer or a sports columnist. He thought about it for a few seconds. "If you love any job and you bring enthusiasm and energy to it, and it's your passion, I don't think you should judge that job on whether it has an impact on the world. I think that doing your job well and better than someone else would've done it has an impact. Some people are butchers and bakers and some people dig ditches and are surgeons. You're going to bring something to it and you're going to make a contribution. If you size up a job by whether I'm having an 'impact' on society, there are very few jobs that meet that test."

We stopped for another red light. He looked over at me and continued. "If you can be a salesman, and you're the best salesman and you love it, and you really feel like you're doing well by your clients, well by your company and well by your family, if that floats your boat, that's great. Other people, it won't float their boats. I don't think there is anything wrong with being a lawyer. It didn't float my boat. I didn't bring joy to it. So I didn't do it as well as I think I could've done it."

He then reflected back to the day he got the call from Memphis' *Commercial Appeal*. As he spoke, Geoff's face glowed with joy. "I can't explain how much fun my job is now. If I won Powerball, I'd show up for work the next day. That's the measurement. I love it every day, everything about it. I love being part of the community. I love having a voice. I can shake things a little bit. I like when people stop me in the grocery store to tell me they liked or didn't like my column. It's an absolute kick."

And now Geoff's dream as a 12-year-old is reality.

REWIND

- Geoff eventually made the leap to journalism because, "I finally understood myself." Once you understand more about yourself, you can get closer to figuring out what you love and need to do. And if the thought you had at age 12 is still with you at age 20 or at age 40 or more, maybe you should listen to it. Especially if your present work is not fulfilling to you and that dissatisfaction is having a Ripple Effect on the rest of your life.

- Geoff also tells us that you can make an impact at any job as long as you bring "enthusiasm and energy to it." I will cover this more in Lesson Eleven, but when you bring joy to a job, it is contagious to others. When you feel good, it helps others feel good. This is a positive Ripple Effect.

- His real world example shows that money is not the only motivator and is definitely not the number one factor for job satisfaction. The negative Ripple Effect was still present even with a Harvard law degree and a six-figure salary. Because Geoff was not living with purpose, "it became a full-scale depression." He ended up choosing $225 a week over six figures. And the risk paid off.

- Geoff was better able to take his career risk because he had a network of supportive people who were conventionally successful, but also loved their jobs. They could sense his well-paying, more conventional profession would not lead him to self-fulfillment. "There was never pressure from my family to be a lawyer. In fact, everyone who knows me said I should not become a lawyer." His parents taught him that work should be a passion, because that is what they experienced in their careers. And his wife's belief in his dream made it easier for him to go out on a limb and take the chance. These people had a positive Ripple Effect.

- Finally, Geoff's story illustrates that the evolution toward living your passion is not an easy one. The journey might take many years and require many sacrifices to accomplish. Yet, once you find your calling, the fire and energy you gain will propel you to achieve incredible results and satisfaction.

CHAPTER FIVE

Depression & Analysis
Making the most out of
your tombstone's dash

In Raleigh, North Carolina, I sat down with Charlie Hinton, a prominent real estate lawyer. We had met briefly once before, during the April 2002 wedding of his daughter, Morgan, to one of my best friends from high school, Bob Lyon. Judging from the lavishness of the wedding festivities, it was obvious that his law career had been a successful one.

The Hintons lived in the same neighborhood as former Democratic Presidential candidate John Edwards. I walked up to their mammoth house nestled amongst large oak and cedar trees. Mr. Hinton greeted me at the door in a button-down business shirt and dress slacks. His grey hair was immaculately parted and his glasses rested comfortably on his nose. A barking chocolate lab immediately relaxed when told to do so. Mrs. Hinton was heading out for tennis as we sat down in the living room. Charlie—he said I could call him Charlie—told me he had a small law practice which was real estate oriented and focused on closings, land development and land purchases. The practice was comprised of three other lawyers and several paralegals and secretaries.

We talked about his career and what law has afforded him to do and see. I was surprised by the tone of his voice. When he described the helicopters, plane trips, sporting events, boats, cars, fishing and hunting trips, he did not use a boastful voice, but a tone one uses when talking about memories. Somber, slow and far away.

In setting up the interview, Morgan told me her dad might talk about a lawsuit. I didn't know what the lawsuit was about and decided I would not ask about it. But, after Charlie talked about the fringe benefits of his career, he brought it up. It was a case that started in 1986 and dragged on for six and a half years.

One of his associates did something without letting the client know and the client sued for malpractice. Charlie had nothing to do with the

case, but because he was the owner of the practice, he was named in the suit. It turned into a long, drawn out malpractice litigation with a lot of peaks and valleys. I was not educated enough in law to grasp the details of partnership disputes, commercial lenders, deeds of trust and legal entities, but Charlie talked about more than six years of trials, tribulations and stress—and a lot of money. "It was a really tough time."

The lawsuit caused him to become extremely dissatisfied with his law career. As he grew more disenfranchised, he met more and more lawyers who felt the same way. Because of this, Charlie became involved with a committee in the bar association focused on analyzing the growing dissatisfaction amongst lawyers. A group of 30 lawyers met and discussed why they wanted to become part of something that would help their peers. Each one detailed their own struggles. "You could hear a pin drop. The stories of what was happening to these lawyers in their practices and how they felt, it was absolutely amazing. People were open and honest about what they were feeling. There were some tears."

That meeting generated enough interest that they formed a task force which ultimately became a committee of the bar association called Lawyer Effectiveness and Quality of Life. This was in 1989, three years after the litigation started. The committee spent a lot of time and money surveying all of the lawyers in North Carolina. The committee members were startled by the responses. "Over 24 percent of us were dealing with symptoms of depression more than two or three times a month. Over 11 percent were thinking about suicide more than once or twice a month. It was shocking."

We talked about why there is so much stress in practicing law. He spoke of a disconnect between what you thought you'd be doing in law school and what you're doing in practice. "You thought you were going to save the world, and you end up doing the drudgery of a real estate practice or a corporate practice where you don't meet many clients and are stuck in an office all of the time. Or, you have clients with higher expectations than what you can do and they are dissatisfied with the results. You have done a good job, but they aren't happy."

The committee found that a lot of people were dissatisfied and depressed. "There were people thinking about killing themselves," he said, louder than before. The ongoing committee work was a good channel for Charlie because it helped take his focus off the litigation. But, the years of trials took a toll on him and he wasn't sure if practicing law was what he really wanted to continue to do. "At some point I started not wanting to go to the office. I wasn't sleeping well. I was tired all the time. I didn't eat and lost 25 or 30 pounds. I was so stressed I thought I was having a heart attack. You don't know what I was dealing with," he said softly.

As one of the researchers for the committee, Charlie started examining what services other organizations offered their members. It was here he made a discovery. "One of the medical doctors we were interviewing said that over 75 percent of doctors who deal with malpractice actions deal with symptoms of depression. The light bulb went on for me. There is a name for all the things I've been dealing with and how I've been feeling all through these years: depression. Even with knowing that, I couldn't really bring myself to accept it."

Eventually, Charlie went to a psychologist, got on some medications and came to grips that he was dealing with depression. He attacked what he was feeling. He also did his best to help others who were battling depression. "It's an illness. We used to treat it as a character flaw, but it's an illness and it can be treated. It's sad. Two-thirds of the people who have depressive illnesses don't seek help. The good side of that is that 80 percent of the people who are treated for depression get significantly better."

Charlie's drive to help others caused him and two other people to form the North Carolina Depressive and Manic Depressive Association. It was a statewide organization to disseminate information about depression and let people know that it's okay to be depressed and get treated for it. He was a driving force behind a 28-episode cable-access show called *Surviving Depression*. He was also part of the group that started Bar CARES (Confidential Attorney Resource and Enrichment Services).

The focus in Charlie's life changed in a lot of ways. "In all of the stress and stuff I went through with the lawsuit and falling into a pit of depression—considering I don't want to do this anymore, feeling like I'm going to be like this forever and I might as well check out—I went through all of that and I realized checking out wasn't the answer."

Suicide is a very personal issue, but I took a deep breath and asked the question. He did not seem to be taken aback or offended. "It's interesting how if you've been scarred by stuff, then it's the scars that give you strength. My dad committed suicide when I was 15. When I was going through the pit I was in, considering how awful it was, I realized suicide wasn't an option because I know what it's like. The questions for those who are left: What, how, and why. There's no way I can do that to my family."

There was a long pause. I spoke first. I told Charlie about the suicide of one my best friends from high school right after graduation. I knew about the scars, the questions and the feelings he was talking about. We sat across from each other and didn't say anything for a few seconds.

Charlie broke the silence. "I spent the majority of my adult life focused more on things, on acquisition, power and money and all of the amenities that come with that. During that rough period of time, even though I was at the bottom, I realized my faith was stronger than I first thought."

His journey for peace came as he gradually moved closer to his faith. At his church, Charlie was around people who weren't the richest or the most powerful in terms of worldly success, but they had a peace about them that he wanted. "Their peace seemed to transcend needing all these other things, and over a period of time, I came to have a closer relationship with God. I had a lot of my success orientation seared away from me. That's not the measure I need to be looking at. It's more of an 'in here' kind of peace (hitting his chest). A peace with your Maker and in the relationships you have with people. Those are the kinds of things that will endure when everything else falls by the wayside."

We then talked again about the boats, and the cars, and the plane flights and the fishing and hunting trips. He had tasted a high level of financial success but then reassessed his values. "I realized that a lot of what I was carrying wasn't the goal and wasn't important. All that quest and running and working all the time, I realized that wasn't what I wanted.

When you really boil it all down, family, friends and relationships are more important than things.

"The way I measured success was how much money I had and how many things I had. It was the outward signs of success and the measurement by our society. That fueled my mental stress and anxiety. Even though I piled up a lot of stuff, I was never going to have enough. That's not necessarily what's going to bring you peace. I had to be seared through some experiences with the lawsuit, facing the possibility of losing millions. Everybody at some point has got to come to peace with themselves," he said and took a deep breath. He sat silent, reflecting.

The dog got up from the floor and stretched as Charlie shifted his weight on the couch. "Where I was headed and where I am now, I realize my run at this is going to be different. I'll stop and smell the flowers and not be so worried about getting to the finish line. I'm going to enjoy the run."

He then talked about something that has stuck with me ever since, "When it's all over and done, when you look at somebody's tombstone you see the date they were born and the date they died and the dash in the middle. The dash in the middle is really your whole life and who you are. There are years of life and relationships and involvements that just boil down to one little snippet. It is sad if the only thing that they can remember about your life is when you were born and died, and the middle is just a dash."

The pace of the conversation slowed, so it was time to wrap it up. I told Charlie I had no idea we were going to be covering the topics we did. He laughed and said, "People are like icebergs. You only see a little top and you don't see what's working underneath. There's a lot more to it."

· · · · · · · · · · · · · · · · · ·

REWIND

- Charlie may be a lawyer, as Geoff Calkins was, but his Ripple Effect is different. He didn't hate his job, he just wasn't happy with what he was valuing. "I spent the majority of my adult life focused more on things, on acquisition, power and money and all of the amenities that come with that." His outward success drive could have contributed to his depression.

  Interestingly enough, it took the negativity of a lawsuit for him to find a new purpose: to help people who were battling depression like he was. "I had to be seared through some experiences..." Charlie began to feel at peace when he shifted his focus from material things to helping people and on family, faith and relationships.

- In addition, unlike Geoff Calkins who grew up with the example of passionate, happy workers who worked well past retirement age, Charlie dealt with the impact of his father's suicide. However, Charlie managed to draw a positive lesson from that and prevented his father's experience from having an unchallenged negative Ripple Effect on his life. Charlie's negative Ripple Effect triggered an analysis that in time, through his dedication to building a support group for others in his field, allowed him to produce a positive Ripple Effect in his own life and that of many of his peers.

- I love what Charlie said about your tombstone, "The dash in the middle is really your whole life and who you are." The question he spurred in me was, What are you going to do with your dash? (See Linda Ellis' poem, *The Dash*)

- Charlie found a cause helping people with depression. I found a cause helping people love their work. Do you have a cause?

LESSON THREE

You Are The One

In my career journey, it took a long time for me to take ownership for whether or not I liked what I did. I was a complainer. I blamed my company, my boss and other people for my dissatisfaction. But once I took personal accountability for my career and for my happiness, the complaining and the blaming were replaced with self-affirmation and focus as I began to interview people and set my itinerary.

Going on the road showed me that I have a say in how I live and work. I have a say in whether or not I am happy. Other people may influence me, but the way I act and feel come down to me.

As I talk about the influence of other people, I would be remiss not to mention the amazing amount of help I've had along the way. I have had supportive family and friends, access to untold amounts of books, research, interviews and a career coach. All of this input helped shape who I am and what I do. But, none of those people or things truly made me into who I am. They shaped me, but I am the one who demanded that I would be passionate about my work and life. I am the one who cashed in my savings to become a Seeker. And I am the one who made the positive and negative choices leading up to today.

On the road of life, you can be guided by other people, by your spiritual beliefs and by education, but, in the end; you are the one who makes choices that impact your life. Other people and experiences may give form to your vehicle, but you are the driver. You decide when to press the gas pedal or hit the brakes. You decide which forks in the road to take. It may seem serendipitous at times (and part of it is), but you decide what you do for work. You decide if you are happy and why.

You decide if you are unhappy and, if so, why. And you decide what plan of action to take.

The sci-fi action movie, *The Matrix*, illustrates this lesson well. The main character, Neo, is plodding away at a job he didn't care about when he gets a phone call. The caller tells Neo he is The One: that he controls the destiny of the world. Neo grapples with the job offer, trying to decide if he really wants to leave his life for a new one. He can try and change the world, or he can stay with stability at a job he doesn't like.

Neo then comes into contact with inspiring people who try to guide him and get him to realize who he is. In one scene, Neo's main mentor, Morpheus, tells him, "I can only show you the door. You're the one that has to walk through it."

It takes Neo many experiences and influences before he finally realizes he is The One. Once he believes he is The One, he goes on to achieve amazing things.

Our journey is like Neo's. On our road, no one is going to tap us on the shoulder and say, "I have the career of your dreams." True, but along the way we encounter guides and navigators. Also, the real world offers us many lessons, if we are listening. Still, for us to truly find our passion and the motivation it takes to reach our goals, we have to take personal accountability to realize that we have the strongest hand in our destiny, and believe that we are The One.

Once we believe we have the personal power to achieve our goals, the steps in the path become much clearer.

The following chapters share stories and advice from people who are living like Neo.

CHAPTER SIX

Become A Life Entrepreneur
Why market penetration, sex and baseball weren't enough

After a weekend with friends at the Ohio Jazz & Rib Fest in Columbus, Ohio, I drove to the sprawling city that is The Ohio State University campus. My dad spent a lot of his career in the supply chain and logistics field and he had set up a lunch interview with Dr. Bud La Londe, Professor Emeritus at Ohio State, a well-known expert in the field. At the Blackwell hotel on campus, a valet took my car and I entered Bistro 2110.

Dr. La Londe arrived in khakis and a white golf shirt with the OSU logo on the arm and the inscription of the logistics program on the chest. Tall and thin with a shaved head, he appeared to be in his 60s. He shook my hand firmly and we spoke for a few minutes about my dad, then ordered lunch.

He began recounting his past in an easygoing manner. He started his career at Ford in manufacturing and then was transferred to work under the VP of Marketing and Sales. "It was a good life until I arrived at the realization that I'd be 55 years old and still a high-priced errand boy. I didn't want to wake up in 20 years still chasing data for the boss. I wanted to get out where the action was."

In the automobile industry, the action is in the field at the dealer level. He joined the Lincoln Mercury regional office and worked his way up while completing his MBA from the University of Detroit. He had been promoted on numerous occasions and was on his way to becoming a major player at Ford. But, things began to change. "I soon got bored by what I was doing. I decided that I didn't really want my boss's job. And I didn't want his boss's job. Once you make that conclusion, you say 'I'm in the wrong place. I don't have the motivation to stick with it and focus.'"

In this period, he looked back on his experiences during his MBA. "Teachers seem to have a very fulfilling life. They read and write and work with bright students. Maybe that's what I'll do."

A few weeks later, he had an epiphany. "The reason I was bored is the people I worked with were only interested in market penetration, sex or baseball, in that order. I am not an intellectual, but I just wasn't getting my jollies. I said there's got to be more. I want to work in a place where I get up in the morning and I'm actually anxious to go to work."

He weighed the options of staying at Ford, starting his own business or entering the academic life. He eventually enrolled at Michigan State for his Ph.D. "I knew I couldn't do good things in an organization where I didn't feel I had a fire in my belly. It wasn't money. I wasn't making as much teaching as I was at Ford. It's never been about money."

The academic life turned out to be the right fit. "I have found it to be exactly what I wanted. Every day you're learning something and you're surrounded by bright people. I smile when I go into the office."

Dr. La Londe's career in academics and business took off. He has accomplished a lot on his way to Emeritus status. He was a full professor at MSU at age 34 and came to Ohio State as a chaired professor in 1969. He was one of the founders of OSU's Global Logistics Program, which is rated as one of the top three in the country. In 1976, he wrote the early standard procedures for customer service. He helped start the Council of Logistics Management, which became the Council of Supply Chain Professionals. In addition, he helped start an educator-practitioner interaction conference that has grown from 20 academics to close to 300 educators from many different countries. He also helped create a doctoral consortium and a well-respected journal of business logistics.

Dr. La Londe has also done his best to pass on the mentorship he received while becoming a professor. He's guided more than 60 students through their doctoral program, thesis and graduation. One student became an assistant secretary of commerce, others have won national awards and he has a shelf full of books written by former students.

"If there is one thing that's been satisfying, it is that you can clone yourself. You try to shape them into your own value set, so that when they go out and work with doctoral students under them, they are able to mentor those people in a way that is productive. It's the ability to do things through people. You need a big lever to make a change in the

world. Well, if you can get 60 bright people and send them out, and they each get 60 bright people and send them out, there is a chance that a change will happen. This is the kind of job where you can do that.

"The real key is that I have my hand on the levers. I run the show. I make all the decisions. I can be a success or a failure, and it all shows. It's all my fault if I do it wrong. This is a business like any other business."

Dr. La Londe surveyed the dining room, then locked his eyes on me. "It's all about managing your own life. You can decide what you want to do. It's like being an entrepreneur, but an intellectual entrepreneur."

He said career choices are not an easy process, but they are choices that each individual has to make. "Carpe Diem. I have this conversation with so many people. 'What should I do? What's my next move?' It's developing your personal strategic plan.

"You have to decide, you have to have the sales bit, planning to work and working your plan. You have to plan your strategy and work your strategy. You've got to work at this," he emphasized.

"I think there are plenty of ways to experiment; the problem is having the resources to experiment and the will to walk away from something. 'I don't like what I'm doing and I don't like what my boss does, so why am I here?' Inertia is a wonderful thing. Once you get a paycheck coming in every week and an apartment and furniture and a car, it takes much more to make a change."

Dr. La Londe has seen how companies, the economy and the workplace have changed. It used to be that there were extensive, company-funded training programs for people. Now it's the responsibility of the individual to learn and grow. "What's happened is the onus for development has shifted from the employer to the employee. Companies are cutting costs by not training people. I recently gave a presentation in Cincinnati and said if you don't spend 15 percent of your time improving yourself and your knowledge base, that you'll be obsolete in five years. And that's probably a conservative estimate.

"You have to retool. What do you know now that you didn't know when you graduated? Soon you'll find you are obsolete."

And becoming obsolete is a difficult situation to be in. "It's like standing up in a leaky canoe. If you move too fast it might tip. At the same time, you eventually know it will sink," he said and moved his body like he was in a tipsy canoe.

"As you get more and more training and education, your number of options goes up, your degrees of freedom increase in terms of scopes of jobs. You need to get your ticket punched."

He hears a lot of complaints from people about lack of training. "'The company isn't developing me.' Well, too bad Joe. You better figure out a way to get it done. You better manage your own life," he said in an authoritative voice.

Dr. La Londe looked at his watch and his expression indicated that our 90-minute talk was more time than he planned to spend. He got up from his chair and laughed. "I didn't want to be concerned with market penetration, sex and baseball. The opportunity to learn is still important to me. I haven't stopped working or stopped thinking." We shook hands and he was off.

. . . .

REWIND

- Dr. La Londe talked a lot about, "managing your own life." He has been successful because he has kept his hands on the levers of his career. He has taken personal responsibility and accountability. "I can be a success or a failure, and it all shows. It's all my fault if I do it wrong."

If you are not satisfied with your work, it is easy to blame others. It is easy to let inertia weigh you down. It takes guts, will and determination to figure out a way to get going in a new direction which you are excited about. You are The One that can do it. You are a life entrepreneur.

Here are some ways to take more ownership of your upcoming career:

- ◊ Interview someone who does what you want to do
  - — Ask them the questions I asked my interviewees
- ◊ Read books pertaining to your anticipated field
- ◊ Take courses that pertain to your projected field
- ◊ Get certified in something that pertains to your desired field
- ◊ Join professional associations that fit your field
- ◊ Subscribe to professional journals and attend conferences in your field
- ◊ Join Toastmasters
- ◊ Sign up for a Dale Carnegie course

CHAPTER SEVEN

Four Jobs by Age 26
All building blocks

As I progressed on my road, colleges asked me to give talks about my interviewees. I also became an adjunct college professor for a year. Many students asked me about "job hopping." I wouldn't recommend a job every three months, but sometimes you have to keep moving to find your niche. Natalie Bongiorno, a nurse who now really likes her job, shows this method in action.

John Jiloty, the editor of *Inside Lacrosse* magazine, set up my interview with Natalie. I drove to Bethesda, Maryland, and walked into the office marked with the sign, "Center for Cancer and Blood Disorders." Natalie, a young, blue-eyed, blonde woman soon came out to greet me. She wore slacks and a red shirt, not the nurse's scrubs I'd expected. She was not the typical family doctor or emergency room nurse. She was a research nurse, a Clinical Research Coordinator.

Because I didn't know what that job title encompassed, she went into fast-paced detail. "This job is very intense. You are constantly a caregiver, whether physically or emotionally." Her organization tries to link up drugs to help cancer patients in two ways. The first is to put cancer patients on new drug regimens that are not yet approved by the FDA. The second is to look at drugs approved by the FDA but not indicated for the specific cancers the patient has. At the time I was there, they had 17 studies underway for varying cancers, including non-Hodgkin's lymphoma, multiple myeloma, lung, breast, ovarian and colon cancers.

"We have a study going right now for chronic myrogenic leukemia where one pill a day puts a patient in complete remission." She radiated energy as she spoke of her work, and especially of the joys of such successes.

Her voice got a little quieter as she talked about the emotional toll when a drug works and helps, but only for a short time. This happened a

lot with what she called solid tumors, such as colon, lung and ovarian cancer. "You can extend their life a couple of months with these drugs."

It hit me that she was working with people who were incredibly sick and dying, not people with the flu. In one area she worked solely with women who had ovarian, cervical, endometrial or uterine cancers, which are very aggressive and normally asymptomatic until the later stages, which means by the time a patient is diagnosed, they are often already at a stage 3C or 4. Stage 4 means it has spread to other organs.

With this group of patients, she dealt with a lot of "Do Not Resuscitate" orders and figured out how the husbands and wives could spend their last months together. "That is hard. Here you see every type of cancer. Each patient affects you differently. I've gotten to the point where I have kind of desensitized myself to a lot of it. If I get upset every time a patient's cancer progresses, I'd be in a mental home. You have to go in there and say let's do this one day at a time. Let's fix this today and come back and see what's going on. There are always a couple of patients that you get attached to. As they start getting sicker you go 'tch, ugghhh!'" She voiced with a deep sigh.

When we met, Natalie was 26 and managed the department of five. Her group looked at targeted therapy drugs, which differ from chemotherapy. Chemo attacks every cell in your system. It really compromises the patient's immune system, usually causing chemo patients to feel very sick. Targeted therapy drugs typically do not have the severe side effects of chemo. "Now they are creating drugs that are targeted to the specific enzymes that are causing the problems with the proteins. We have some drugs that are called anti-angiogenesis drugs. They literally shut off the blood supply to the tumor. They are receptor specific," she explained.

Her team has worked on a vaccine study where they remove someone's cancerous lymph node, send it off to a lab and then prepare a vaccine from the lymph nodes. "When that vaccine is put in, the body is able to identify what's foreign right away and your antibodies kick in. This is different from waiting until the cancer is at a level where you can see it on a scan. It grabs it when it is actually on a cellular level and we can identify what the problems are."

They also worked on a lymphoma and multiple myeloma study called leukapheresis, which pulls out the patient's blood and spins it down to separate white cells from plasma and red cells. T cells are then extracted from the white cells. A unit of that is re-infused with the blood and transfused back into the patient. The T cells are then sent to a company where they add two enzymes which are missing in the patient. The enzymes stimulate the T cells, increasing the count from five million to five billion. "They create these five banks of T cell-enriched blood and a month later they are shipped back to us to re-infuse into the patient and hopefully put them in remission."

Natalie's career path started off in psychiatric nursing but during her internships and clinicals (onsite work with patients), she discovered that she did not want to be a hands-on nurse in a hospital environment. "I had done the med-surg floor and I didn't want to be physically lifting people and moving them."

She almost left the nursing field altogether, but the staff persuaded her to stick with it because her nursing degree would offer her a lot of options. She was able to see the industrial side of nursing during an internship at Procter & Gamble Company. Her job was to assess the work environment of a specific group of employees and figure out what she could do to promote healthier lifestyles.

Natalie did her final internship working in the clinic of a large John Deere plant in Illinois. She was the only nurse on site and practiced occupational health. She conducted all of the employees' physicals, giving appropriate shots and was the first responder to heart attacks and manufacturing accidents that occurred in the plant. She also learned case management from the business side, which meant trying to use the most cost effective treatment.

After graduating with her BSN and RN, at 21, she went back to her hometown of Milwaukee, Wisconsin, and got a job as a cancer research nurse for a large, private practice with 10 offices. "I created research departments in each office with each doctor. I loved it. That's my thing, I'm kind of go, go, go. Every day I was reacting to something and learning something new about the disease process or something in the research world. You just have to jump in and figure it out."

At 23, Natalie had a desire to move to a new city. She was working on her MBA, but shifted the focus to a master's in research administration. After some online investigation, she moved to the Washington, DC area and enrolled at George Washington University. By the time you read this, she'll be done with her MSHS (Master of Science in Health Sciences) in clinical research administration.

Her first job in DC was at a cardiology practice. "That was a means to an end. I was not embracing the cardiac world." Her goal was research and she got a job doing just that in Gynecological Oncology, but it left her working off by herself, which was not a good fit for someone who was so clearly a "people person."

"I started this job a few months ago. Doesn't it sound like I've had 10 million jobs?" She laughed. "Every job was a building block."

She loves nursing, but does not claim that it is an easy field. "It's a ton of work, but there are a lot of options people don't know about. Nursing allows you to use your critical thinking skills. It's very autonomous and nurses have a lot of authority. A lot of times they are the ones with the patients 24 hours a day. They are the ones telling the doctors what's going on with the patients, and then together, assessments and decisions are made concerning how the patients are to be treated.

"The job is very intense. Regardless of what area you choose, the nursing field is very emotional. Even in a business setting, you're working with people who are always very vulnerable and coming to you because they need you for something. You are always taking care of people."

Her energetic personality seems to fit well with her career choice. "You have to be able to multitask and do 15 things at once. However, you also have to be very patient, compassionate and caring. You need to have that emotional side but also need to be strong and be able to think quickly on your feet. It only takes three minutes to mess something up. You are in trouble if you're not able to identify a critical lab or if you don't call somebody in a timely fashion.

"But, it's very rewarding. Having people say, 'Thanks, I could not have gotten through this without you; you made this process okay for me, you made me feel safe.' That's the best part of it."

Then she talked about some of her non-work friends. "When they say they had such a horrible day at the office, I want to say 'What??? You don't even know what a bad day is.' Spend some time in my infusion room and watch how sick those patients are and then come back and put it in perspective. Tell me that you feel sorry for yourself because your boss was mean to you today. Who cares, you're not dying," she said louder than I had heard her speak all day.

Her daily experiences with life and death give Natalie a unique perspective on career and the choices which are available. "Don't stay in a career if you are not happy or completely content with it. I would tell people not to wait. If they are unhappy, quit complaining and actually do something about it.

"I have no regrets. If I were to die tomorrow, that's fine. I've done everything I've wanted to do. I wanted to move. I moved. Within a few weeks I had a job. I wanted to go to school and I'm doing it. Granted I'm on my fourth job and I'm 26, but those jobs were all building blocks. This is where I want to be right now. Instead of worrying about 10 years from now, I am focused on right now because this is all that matters. I am lucky; I love what I am doing."

She shook her head and looked out the window. "You figure it out. It will work out. Everyone has so many excuses for why they can't do it, but then they complain for the next 10 years. You have control over everything that you do. For the most part you can determine what your path is going to be. If you don't take the initiative to pursue it, there is no one else to blame," she said passionately.

As Natalie took a breath, one of her co-workers knocked on the door and said a patient needed to see her.

REWIND

- Natalie has had four jobs by age 26. So what? For now she has found the right fit. She is using her education, personality and passion to the max. "Every job was a building block."

  In every job that you have, no matter what it is, you will learn something. Your learning will show you what you like and what you don't. You will learn about yourself, about people, about your field, about management style or about an industry—but you will learn.

- The work of Natalie and her group helps extend the lives of cancer patients and may even cause them to go into remission. At the same time, many of their patients don't make it. Natalie shows that a person can love a job that takes an emotional and stressful toll.

- If you are not happy with your work, as Natalie says, it's on you. "Quit complaining and actually do something about it." This doesn't mean quit your job tomorrow. It means tomorrow is the day you begin the steps to get on a new path—your path.

CHAPTER EIGHT

Quit Faking It
Finding your own reasons to believe

Growing up, I always thought of my older cousin Kevin, as an artist. He wasn't selling paintings when I was young, but whenever our families would get together, he was always drawing or playing his guitar. My history with Kevin, who is seven years older than I am, runs deep. He and his brother, Colin, are like older brothers to me. I went to their football games when they were in high school. They took me with them to parties. Kevin was the first person I knew who had a tattoo. At a family get together, I took my parents aside and asked them why Kevin had long hair and an earring. They told me Kevin was part of the "Rainbow People" and trying to "find himself." As a thirteen-year-old, I had no idea what that meant.

After a long road of his own, Kevin has found himself. He is now a professional artist living in Charleston, South Carolina. He paints pictures in his own style; a style I've seen a magazine refer to as "distorted reality." I can best describe it as a scene looked at through a fish eye lens. Kevin's art is not limited to canvas. He is also a photographer, video editor, graphic designer and moviemaker. He is the new breed of artist, one who uses multi-media to convey their view of the world.

We talked about his career journey at his newly completed art studio; a dimly-lit, two-story metal building in the shape of a half moon located in his back yard. Kevin stood in front of his easel and brushed and dabbed on a commission of a downtown Charleston scene as we chatted. His cameras and video-editing equipment were set up in the back corner of the room. The creative vibe was enhanced by the scent of burning incense and the sound of soft jazz music in the background.

Kevin first sensed being drawn to art as a teenager. While waiting in a doctor's office, he leafed through some magazines and saw an article

about an artist in New York City. They showed the artist standing next to one of his paintings. "It struck me. I wondered what steps he had to take just to have that picture in this magazine, in order to be good enough, to be recognized, where somebody would like his art enough to buy it. I didn't figure anything out that day, but I definitely think back on that moment now. It's ironic, because now I've had my pictures in very similar magazines."

Kevin always dabbled in drawing, but did not pick up a paintbrush until he was 22, at school in Charlotte, North Carolina. "I knew I wanted to be an artist. I always fantasized about it." A full time art career did not just materialize for Kevin. He had to work to pay the bills. He started working in computer graphics at a TV station in Charlotte. At one of the stations, he met his future wife, Cathy. In 1997 they moved to Charleston where an accounting software company hired him to do graphics. His role was to work on the visuals for their new customer training software.

Kevin worked full time for the software company, but still painted and dabbled in other media on the side. After a few years, he began to resent his job. The corporate environment did not fit with his personality or artistic goals. "I was working at this white-collar factory. The whole time, all that was going through my head was how can I get out of this situation? I can't believe I have to waste my time here. I have to go into this job and pretend that I care about what these people are saying, sitting around these meetings talking about ways of making this meaningless task better," he said, taking his focus off the easel.

During his time at the software company, his paintings began to generate buzz around Charleston. In 2002 he and another artist, John Duckworth, had their work scheduled for a gallery opening. Rather than having a traditional event, they took a risk and staged The Entropy Show, a huge, fictional protest.

Because of our family ties, I was among the Charleston crowd of hundreds at The Entropy Show. Planted picketers stood outside the gallery, marching in circles holding signs reading "More March Scenes," "Save Rainbow Row" and "Get out of Charleston." Television news crews captured the climax: a slow moving parade of limos carrying the artists and their entourages flanked by security guards. All hell broke loose upon Kevin and John's arrival. The picketers berated the artists, the crowd yelled for the sake of yelling and the artists scribbled autographs as they were whisked inside the gallery. The Entropy Show was a hit.

One of the people in the crowd later saw the film Kevin made of The Entropy Show and took it to the higher-ups of GMR Marketing, a group in Chicago that was kicking off a new product for Unilever, Axe Body Spray. In May of 2002 they asked Kevin to create a similar buzz at Axe Body Spray's product launch meeting. "I started making videos for this project. I worked my regular job during the day and spent the rest of my time editing at home, shooting scenes, staying at friends' houses, running back and forth shooting and editing it further, staying up until sometimes 5 or 6 a.m. and then getting up and going to work at 8:30 a.m. and then doing it all over again," he said excitedly all in one breath. They did all of the shooting, editing and videos very quickly, in less than a month.

"I felt like this was my ticket." The feeling of pointlessness was gone. "A recurring thought a lot of artists have is that we're on to something or we've just figured something out. It's that kind of excitement from within that pushes you. When you get that feeling, you feed off of it and use it like fuel. Almost like a mad scientist. You rub your hands together going 'Oh boy, here it comes. Whoa, wait until they see this one!'" He had set down his brush to gesture and play the part.

2002 was a whirlwind. "I was in a constant state of excitement." The Axe Body Spray project went better than planned and Kevin began to do more with all aspects of his art. He was still working at the software company and, because his job was still getting done, his boss gave him leeway. But, after a few months, the powers that be spoke to Kevin's boss. "They said I was spending too much time doing my art. They wanted people going home with nothing on their minds other than thinking about what they could do to better their work tasks. That makes sense, but if you don't have a true passion for what you're doing, it is hard to do that."

Eventually it got harder and harder for him to play the game. He and Cathy talked about art as a full-time career. "I decided to stop faking it and planned my exit strategy. June 7, 2002 was my last day."

He paced in front of the canvas, talking to me in an animated tone. "Life is hard. You have to find your own reasons to believe. Until you do that, you're going around on someone else's theory of life. There is nothing wrong with that, but eventually you need to come up with your own reasons to live, your own philosophy of life. You have to have that burning thing going that you're on to something."

We agreed that, unfortunately, a lot of people go through life wanting that feeling, but never really getting it. And even more painful, some people have the burn but don't pursue it. "If you feel something deep down, you have to trust your instincts. That's not easy. As an artist, I kind of always somehow knew it was in there. It was almost to the degree of being a narcissistic weirdo. I actually used to fantasize about when the world would realize I was a genius. That sounds horrible to say, but my thinking was: 'Wait until those bastards find out. They have no idea what's about to hit them.'"

He said the dream is to get paid to do things you would do for free in the first place. "If anybody can take what they do, take their strengths, perfect it and it is recognizable as theirs; that is the answer. Even if I had to go back and start working at a job I'm miserable doing, I'd still be painting and shooting and editing. Even if I wasn't making any money at it, I'd still be doing my thing."

Kevin has hit his stride and we talked about how others could find theirs. "Whatever you're doing, you need to be doing it because you feel it in your gut, not because it's what you've been told all your life you should be doing. I was lucky; art was just something I did. I did it for free. I did it to get away from what I was doing, my job. I'd look forward to getting off work so I could go paint or shoot or edit. Now, it is the work," he said with a smile.

• •

REWIND

- Kevin said, "I kind of always somehow knew it [being an artist] was in there." But it took many years for his desire to turn into a reality that paid the bills. In the process, he tried to live the life of a steady paycheck at a corporation. That was acceptable for a time, but he eventually "had a feeling he was on to something." That feeling fueled him to work insanely long hours doing his full time job during the day and his art at night and into the wee hours of morning. That worked out until he was forced to choose between the two. "You have to find your own reasons to believe." He took his own advice and ventured out on his own in multi-artistic realms.

- Kevin's story conjures up a few questions:

  ◇ What is burning inside of you that can be used as fuel?

  ◇ What can you get paid for that you'd do for free?

  ◇ What if you have a burning passion for something and can't take the leap as Kevin did? I don't think you should just turn off your talent and bury your passion. You say, okay, this may not be a full-time thing for me, but how can I live my passion, even if it is in small doses?

  ◇ Is it acceptable for you to use your gifts and have other people make money from it? If you're okay with that, you may be able to find work in numerous arenas. If not being your own boss bothers you and you need to control your own destiny, you had better put your sales and marketing hat on and start figuring out how to get paid.

LESSON FOUR

Who Are You?

I carried a very strange feeling with me during the first four years of my career: "I don't like my job, but I have no clue what else I want to do." And I'll tell you what, it's tough to be in that situation. "I'm not happy, but I have no direction for what's next."

The road gets easier when you know what you want to do because then you can begin a plan of attack to help get there. In actuality, the core goal of quitting my job to travel the country interviewing people was to answer the questions: Who am I? What is my purpose? What do I want to be?

I have since learned there are millions of us waking up each day going to a job we don't love, but at the same time, without having a true understanding of what would make us happy. That state of indecision eats away at you.

I have learned that each of us is born with natural talents and abilities. Yet, we don't always know what they are, how to tap into them or how to apply them to work. The key for happiness and success is to take advantage of who you already are rather than being someone you are not.

In order to take advantage of who you are, you have to do some self-analysis. When I give talks on this topic, I tell people, "If you ask questions, a road will begin to unfold. If you do nothing, nothing will change."

I wrote an article for *Next Step* magazine where I listed these ten helpful questions:

- What am I naturally good at?
- What are my strengths and weaknesses?
- When am I energized?
- What classes do I (or did I) enjoy the most?
- What classes are (or were) easier to work hard in?
- What type of work do I constantly put off?
- What (strengths, desires, potential) do the people in my inner circle see in me?
- When I have to work, what do I enjoy doing?
- What do I like to do outside of school/work?
- What type of mark do I want to leave?

There are also career and personality assessments that you can take. These are an invaluable way to help you see your natural predispositions. Each one will help answer different questions.

I am not going to recommend one assessment over another. You may be able to take free assessments via your school's guidance office/career center or your city's career center. Or you can Google "career and personality assessments" and find a ton of them. These may not be free, but they will help you get some unbiased answers.

Please understand, although these tools will give you general areas to think about, they are only partial assessments, and may change as you change. Don't pigeonhole yourself because of what they say. The assessments provide great information, but they are just one piece of the puzzle.

Another way to learn how you feel about a career is to experience it. Here is a list of potential ways to see what a job is like:

- Go listen to a speaker in your area of interest
- Reach out to your alumni networks for information
- Seek out and interview people in the field
    - ◇ Ask them the questions I asked my interviewees
- Take a class
- Shadow someone who does what you want to do
- Do an internship in the field
- Volunteer in the field you'd like
- Work part time in the field
- Work a few hours for free in the field

The chapters in this lesson offer examples and advice for those who don't know what they want to do. Once we know who we are, it makes it easier to know what type of job we'd like.

CHAPTER NINE

What If I Don't Know What I Want to Do?

Expert advice

As my journey progressed and I was asked to give talks, I connected with CareerBuilder's VP of Human Resources, Rosemary Haefner. As someone who helps career searchers on a daily basis, I knew her input would be essential.

We started by talking about the masses of people who are not satisfied by their work. Rosemary also referred me to CareerBuilder's quarterly employment forecast, *The Pulse*. Some of the stats I found at that time were startling:

- Nearly half of the American workforce did not look forward to going to work

- Six in ten workers planned to change jobs annually

- One in five workers was actively looking for a new job on a weekly basis

- Over 14 million people were online each week looking for jobs

Millions of us are at jobs we are not passionate about and I wanted to know the reasons why. Rosemary said, "Believe it or not, most people don't take the time to sit and think about what they want to do. We're very much programmed to take a job to have a job. A paycheck to have a paycheck."

And that is a quote I use often in my talks. When I graduated from college, there was no job or field that interested me. That part is somewhat acceptable. What is not acceptable is that I had put in no effort to find a job that would interest me.

I had no plan. I did no research in college or afterwards. I was programmed to just go and find a job because it was the time to find a job. If I had done some research on what drove me and what didn't, I would've tried to create a plan where work fit my personality and drove my passions. Instead, I followed my brother into sales and started collecting a paycheck.

Also while I was in school, I only saw broad fields like sales, marketing, advertising and public relations as options. Other people may see medicine, law, education, etc. as the only realistic options. What I know now that I didn't know then is there are a lot of niche jobs that allow you to live your passions. You just have to hunt for them or figure out a way to create the job you want.

Rosemary said many of us don't know what we want to do. But she also said many of us are like I was. We don't know what we want AND we don't try and figure it out. We just remain in this inert state of not knowing. I brought up a class at Harvard that I had heard of that dealt with self-actualization (I will explain more about this in Chapter 12). This is a class that teaches you to figure out what you like and what you don't. What motivates you and what de-motivates you.

"It is encouraging to hear the self-actualization course is available. That is not something typical within a degree program. Many times you have to seek that out on your own."

I know that during my undergraduate and graduate school, I took no class that focused on figuring out what motivated me and what didn't. More and more colleges are trying to incorporate these types of classes. If Harvard is teaching their students about self-actualization, there must be something to it.

For those of us who didn't have a self-actualization course, we have to do it on our own. Rosemary's advice on this is twofold. "First, you need to sit, think, be very honest with yourself and be very introspective. That will show you some things.

"Secondly, the best way to get what we call 'data points' is by talking to others about what they see in you. Ask family, friends, coaches and teachers about your personality. You need them to be brutally honest. Is there a common theme about certain personality traits that you have? What would they say you are passionate about? What would they say about your personality and careers? Then take those answers and figure out how to match them with different opportunities at work."

Another option is to use a career coach. I have used one and know many people who do. They act as a sounding board and advice giver. "Being coached gives you an objective observer who listens to what you say and reflects back to you what they hear. And they are not going to put any biases on it."

I realize not everyone can afford a career coach. An alternative is to find people to talk with about you and your career road. Find people who can be objective and provide you with brutally honest feedback. What you don't want is the well-intentioned answer of, "You'll be great at anything."

Prepare yourself for them to be brutally honest. They may tell you things you might not like hearing.

As an example, if you say you want to be a veterinarian but that you also hate blood and you've nearly failed out of your biology and science classes, your confidant should tell you that being a vet is probably not the best fit. Your next step would be to ask, "How can I parlay my passion for animals into work that doesn't involve the scientific aspect?" If I were one of your chosen advisors, I might encourage you look at different jobs within the veterinary field: administration, marketing, communications, public relations, lobbying and so forth. Or, you might forget the medical aspects and work with animal training, pet photography, breeding uncommon animals or the business side of an animal rescue organization. One of these choices might allow you to live your passion for animals in a way that takes advantage of your strengths.

It's all about knowing yourself better. Step one is to evaluate your personality and passions on your own. Step two is to find people close to you and talk with them about what they see in you. If you can do what you are naturally designed to do, you'll be better at it and happier doing it. And, by being happier, you'll perform better, which will make you happier... (See how it snowballs!)

As I mentioned in the lesson introduction, another way to get to know yourself better is by taking personality profiles and psychological tests. The information you can garner from these is great, but you need to keep it in perspective. Rosemary said, "A lot of the tests say there is this bucket of careers that you should focus on, which is good. They give you a general area in which the likelihood is greater you'll feel comfortable and then succeed."

Still, she also cautioned, "Tests are one data point and an interesting one, but I wouldn't put all my eggs in that basket. The risk for people is that they could take a test and it will become the be all and end all. 'That's my map and if I follow, it will lead me to nirvana'. You need to be realistic. The results are interesting but you can't live or die by them."

I have seen some of my friends and students lock in on their career choices because of their profile and test results, and not see that the results are just one piece of the puzzle. They say, "I really hate my major, but XYZ tests say this field is a good fit for me."

Then they focus on something they don't like, sometimes putting up the blinders and missing out on potential options that may be a better fit. If you don't know what you want to do, then the tests may help provide some guidance that we can't always provide for ourselves. But, if the tests point you in a direction and you try it and it doesn't feel right, listen to yourself. You know your own responses better than any test does.

After test profiles, we discussed career changes. I told her that I was a perfectionist and that I felt like a failure for not enjoying my sales career. She said, "I would encourage people to do self-actualization activities at all points of their career. People should be realistic. You're probably not going to crack that code and figure it all out on the first try. And you know what? That's okay."

It is important for us to know that if we haven't cracked the code, we can still try. "It's become a lot more common and acceptable that individuals are going to change jobs and change career fields quite a few times during their life. And that's more than acceptable."

It is good to know we can try to crack the code, but Rosemary said many of us stop our search before it starts. "A lot of people say they want to see what the next great fit is, but it can't be in financial services and it can't be in health care and it can't be in this or that. They already have all of these disclaimers on it. It's what you're open to.

"It is a very difficult thing to find the job that is going to be wonderful and where you're never going to have a problem. You don't have to be happy with your job all of the time. You can learn a lot from problems. You need to be open-minded about what is a potential fit."

That makes sense. The people I interviewed love what they do, but they still have ups and downs at work just like everyone else. It's just that their highs far outweigh their lows.

Rosemary hears a lot of complaints about companies and bosses. They have a role in our satisfaction, but it's on us, too. "There are a few things a company should be offering you: training, constant feedback, fair compensation, etc. But those things are never going to be enough to make you completely happy all of the time. It's a two-way street for an individual to be happy. It's not just 'What is everybody doing for me at this company.' You need to be actively participating and need to know what you're trying to get out of work."

To know what you are trying to get out of work, you need to ask yourself some questions and blend your personality to your job. It is even better if your employer can assist you in this process. "People and companies both need to take the time to go through the exercise of finding jobs that are a match. People will always be more motivated when they have a better fit."

REWIND

Are you like almost half of the American workforce who, on a regular basis, do not look forward to going to work? If so, maybe now is a good time to analyze what factors go into your dissatisfaction:

- Is it the nature of the job which is a bad fit with your talents and aspirations? Then you may need an entire career overhaul.

- Is only part of the job not the right fit? If so, is there a way to keep, or do more of, what you like while reducing what you don't?

- Is it the right kind of job in the wrong company culture? If so, time to job hunt!

- Are you working for a company with a good culture and a general mission that is the right fit, but you're in the wrong role or department? If so, think about the role you wish you could do day in and day out. In a careful way, can you talk with someone about switching roles or departments within the company? (Even if it means a cut in pay for the time being?)

Again, if you are struggling and searching for the right career, take the time to think about these areas:

- Stop and think about your personality traits: Do some self-exploration
    ◇ Quiet yourself and think about what you are good at and what you enjoy doing.
    ◇ Take a career/personality test.
    ◇ Get "data points" from others about your personality and potential.

- Match your personality to your career and the company whose job offer you accept.
    ◇ Think about the culture of a company before you go there.

- Chances are good you won't figure it out on the first try, and that is okay. Learn from all the experiences work and life offers.

CHAPTER TEN

There Are Numerous Correct Answers

Personality and branches

People who spend their careers analyzing people and society can gain helpful insights into the career journey. I sat down with Bob Ford in Port Orange, Florida. He had retired as the city's police chief and currently taught criminology at the University of Central Florida.

Bob's path wove between policing and education. He went to college at Niagara University, where an engaging criminology professor got Bob past the frustrations that often come with the early learning stages of a new subject. "I've found out most things in life are quite interesting after you break the initial barriers." His accent was strong evidence of his upbringing in Long Island, New York.

Criminology fit Bob well. "I really enjoy learning and understanding the social sciences in general. What makes people tick? How do societies operate? Criminology has an interesting vantage point on these areas, so I enjoyed the materials."

After Niagara, Bob began graduate school at the University of Illinois, in Urbana. There he took part in a Law Enforcement Assistance Administration project for two years, which allowed him to ride the streets with the Chicago Police Department. The goal of the project was to give educators experience on the streets. "This type of project was rare then, and it is now," Bob explained.

He found the streets exciting and interesting, but was still drawn to the academic world. Upon graduation he took a job teaching criminology at SUNY Buffalo in 1969.

The timing was not great. "It was my first year teaching and it was a very tumultuous time in society. There were riots, which caused the student body and the faculty to be very much gripped in turmoil." After two years of teaching, he left and got back into the police field. He took

a job as the chief deputy, third in command, at Buffalo's Erie County Sheriff's Department.

"Biochemically, I am not pre-disposed to be a professor. I like the give and take of a moving environment rather than a contemplative one."

Bob enjoyed classroom teaching, but not sitting at a desk hour after hour writing analytical articles. "I can do it, have done it and have had articles published, but it's not something I enjoy. It's a real annoyance."

The chief deputy job had a good mixture of problem solving and crisis management. "Policing is a fascinating job because you never know what's going to walk in the door. It's always active. It has constant movement. There is always something different occurring."

After close to seven years, Bob took a job serving the city as commis-sioner of Buffalo's Metro Police. Three years later, he applied for and became the police chief of Port Orange, Florida, a city of 50,000. He was chief there for 13 years until he retired at the age of 55 and went back to teaching.

"Policing is a whole different world. I tell this to my criminology students. When I was chief, I thought everyone in Port Orange was drunk by four o'clock in the afternoon because after four o'clock everyone I met was drunk. Well, when you have that selected view of life and all that you see is the disadvantaged of the world, it is easy to become extremely jaded. I tried to change the vantage point of the officers, which was a very difficult thing to do. I enjoyed the challenge. It was always interesting."

Now, as a professor working with young people, he deals with a lot of students trying to figure out what they want to do. Bob emphasized two main points: matching your personality to your job and having proper expectations. And when Bob emphasizes he cuts to the chase.

"I tell my students, you've got to tie a job to your personality. The focus is to clearly understand what the hell they like to do and what they don't like to do," he bellowed. "That's where the nexus (connection) comes. It's got to fit who you are and what you're interested in. To do that, you've got to know yourself. One of my strengths is I know myself. Even if I'm fooling other people around me by impression management, I have yet to be able to fool myself. Sometimes life would be a lot easier if you could bullshit yourself too," he laughed.

"Know what works for you and start looking for a fit. There are a couple of matrices I look at: stress and people. Some people cannot stand crises. If that's you, it's very important you take a job that isn't a highly stressful one. The need for working with other people is another issue. Some people love it, some hate it. Trial and error. You figure this out as you get older and after you make mistakes; which is a stupid way to do it," he said and laughed again.

Bob's message echoed Rosemary Haefner's: you need to start by examining what you like to do and what you don't.

The conversation then shifted to whether there is only one job or field that will fit. Bob thought the answer was no. "I think we all have a lot of callings. You are on a road with a lot of branches and probably 80 percent of the branches are acceptable. It all depends on your personality. If you hate reading and writing, you don't want to become an attorney. If you don't like dealing with people, there's a bunch of jobs you shouldn't take."

Bob had an interesting point about how skills can be applied across industries. "Managing is managing. Does that differ if you are running the finances of a utility company or a police department? Ninety percent of my work as police chief was managing 100 employees. My biggest issues were sick time, promotions, petty fights between people, motivating certain employees, slowing others down and organization. I could've been building a road. There is a great deal of similarity in all of this."

Bob then added another insight. "When you do know what fits, you need to ask, how do you get there? That's as big a question as the first. How does it really operate? What are its real demands? And then you've got to put those together and see how they sync up with you."

He illustrated part of that by explaining that many of his students want to become criminal investigators (CSI) and FBI agents. "Right now there is no structured way for 90 percent of them to achieve that. The only way you become an investigator today is to become a police officer and then get promoted to that assignment. I have all sorts of students who have decided they want to be CSI. There must be 300 or 400 jobs in the country and 50,000 people applying. It's a bad mix. You've got to know the system."

He returned to talking about his teaching and some of the pitfalls he sees with his students. "I am teaching ethics right now. One of the questions I ask is to think about what they want as a goal. Where are they going? What do they want out of life? You can make your life absolutely freakin' miserable by having goals that are inconsistent with what you're going to get. You've got to plan for where you're going.

"And I'm not just talking about jobs. You can apply this to missions and lifestyles. Life is not only about work. It's also about building a structure of existence that you can be happy with.

"Secondly, people are way out of line on the real world. They tell me, 'We're not going to dress in suits and ties.' You have to decide what your priorities are and what you're willing to give up in order to get something else. Life is about strategic compromises."

I laughed when he told me about suits and ties. In college, I was the guy who would've said there was no way I'd be wearing a suit. Yet, for two out of my first three sales jobs, I had to wear a suit and tie every day. I didn't like it, but I compromised. And, in the end, having to wear a suit was not the reason I left sales. I still wear a suit when it serves to help me get my message and information out to those who need it!

On the career road, we may have to make strategic compromises to get us to where we want to go. You can have preferences, but don't close yourself off; you may miss out an opportunity.

Bob's police chief bellow again emphasized the importance of personality. "Our personality dictates what we will be both very happy and very unhappy at. Within that there is a range of options and sometimes luck will determine which option you end up with. Luck is going to be a factor in everyone's life, but we can influence the roll of the dice.

"The equation is understanding yourself honestly and what makes you tick, what motivates you, and what you like to do. Also to understand the little things that frustrate you and the things that give you joy on a daily basis. Once you begin to understand that, you are on your way."

• • • • • • • • • • • • • • • • • • • •

REWIND

- Sitting down with Bob reaffirmed the importance of matching jobs to personality. As he said, "To do that, you've got to know yourself."

  To know yourself, determine what you like to do and what you don't. Look at Bob's matrices of stress and people. And examine your goals.

- Bob said, "Managing is managing." It is true that you can take your skills and use them in various capacities across industries and organizations. Yet, I would add that it helps to believe in the core mission of the organization where you work. Bob enjoyed the sociological aspect of police work and, therefore, enjoyed managing his officers.

- After listening to the recording of my interview with Bob and writing this chapter, some of his other insights really rang true for me. He said, "You are on a road with a lot of branches and probably 80 percent of the branches are acceptable."

  At one point, I was solely focused on being an author. But, like his students wanting to be CSI, I didn't realize how publishing worked. For the most part, you just don't become an author. This became an extreme frustration for me because I could only see one path to success.

  Eventually, I realized that my desire to write and have a positive influence on others could be accomplished in other ways. I became a speaker and college professor. I wrote a business book on innovation and became communications director for a company. I eventually hit my goal of being an author, but these branches were strategic compromises that fit my personality, taught me a lot, and expanded my career road.

If you have a passion for something, ask yourself if there are any strategic compromises you can make. Remember, there are numerous acceptable branches that can fit your personality and allow you to live your passion.

CHAPTER ELEVEN

How Do I Know My Decision is Right?

Questions + Research = Confirmation

Many people tell me I was courageous to leave my job and go on the road. I'm not sure about all of that. When I think about courage and conviction, I think of my distant cousin, Lisa Caynor, and her husband, Rick. I sat down with them inside an old church that had been converted into a home in Harrisburg, Pennsylvania.

Their life is an example of what happens when you ask questions and then act on the answers. I risked some things to do what I did, but when I sat down with Rick (34) and Lisa (33), they told me about a risk much greater than mine. They were in the process of moving their life and two children, Kristin (11) and Ricky (9), to Thailand to start a missionary program called City on a Hill.

My family had previously told me about Rick's powerful story of becoming a missionary. Our lives had started quite differently. I went to church with my parents and attended Sunday school. Growing up, Rick didn't know what the inside of a church looked like. I was in accelerated classes. He went to jail in middle school. I grew up in a "Leave it to Beaver" household. He was raised by a family who dealt marijuana and crack cocaine. At the time of our interview Rick's father and two brothers were in jail.

As we talked, Rick used a term he referred to as "markers." Markers are those things you look back on and identify as signposts when you finally feel that everything that has happened for years and years has brought you to a crucial point. Markers lead to a culmination.

The first marker in Rick's life happened when he was 15 and living in the state of Washington. While standing on the street with a group of his friends, a guy they knew drove up asked if anyone wanted to go to a Christian concert. "I didn't know what Christian meant, but I wanted to go to a free concert."

Lisa's parents (Dale and Susie), Lisa, Rick, Kristin, and Ricky

They drove to Seattle for the show and Rick liked the music. They sang about God and Jesus. "If someone came up to me at that point and said, 'Rick, who is Jesus Christ?' I could not have told you anything about Him. I was thinking, who is this guy?"

At the end of the show the bands read verses Romans 5:8 and Corinthians 5:17 from the Bible, which referred to mistakes, starting anew and that old sins are in the past. "I thought, 'You know what, if God can offer me a new life through Jesus Christ, I want it. I don't want what I have now.'"

He laughed when I asked if his transformation was immediate. "There was an instantaneous change, but it wasn't like in a movie. It wasn't, 'Okay, I'm a Christian now, and everything is hunky dory, I no longer have any problems and everything is fine.' It wasn't like that. The funny thing is, it's not like that even now. It's a process of growing closer and closer to Him. It's a transformation. It's ongoing."

Rick started to study the Bible and by the time he finished high school, he had met his future wife, Lisa, and ended up enrolling at a Christian Bible College. "All I knew was that I wanted to serve God."

At 19, he went on his first mission trip to Romania with one of his professors. They traveled through Germany, Austria and Hungary, staying with other missionaries along the way. "They talked about how they were giving their lives to the Lord by serving other people. I had a great time and saw a vibrant faith that I'd never seen before. I remember coming back home with the conviction that missionary work was what God wanted me to do."

When he returned from Europe, he discussed with Lisa the possibility of doing long-term missionary work, since they already served together in the Youth Ministry at their church. They concluded that they should wait. Since returning from Europe, he has gone on short mission trips to most of Western and Eastern Europe, Mexico, Japan, Thailand, Bangladesh and India. "That was another marker. All those trips I had taken over twelve years, all the training, it was preparing me to do exactly what I'm doing right now."

Like many non-missionaries, I quizzed them about the money factor in their line of work. They both laughed. "You don't go into this to make a lot of money," Rick said. In unison, they said, "This pays an eternal dividend." Lisa laughed and told me about a sign her grandfather has, "Working for the Lord doesn't pay much, but the retirement plan is out of this world."

Rick works with a lot of young people and they ask him two main questions: What is my purpose? What does God want me to do?

"What I tell them is there are a lot of factors that go into that. How has God made you and your personality? What you enjoy and what you're good at? The abilities, the passion, the desire. There must be a reason for your desire. I pose this question to them, and we ask it of ourselves often.

"What can you do in your life that will pay the highest dividends? Not financial dividends, but, number one, what can you do that at the end of your life, where you are going to say, 'I didn't waste it,' and number two, what is going to give you the highest return for the things that are really important?"

As a teacher, Lisa is asked the same questions. She answers, "Don't take what you've been given; your abilities, your talents, your love, whatever it is; don't take what you've been given and bury it."

Rick and Lisa believe that they are using the abilities and passions they've been given by going to Thailand to start and run the City on a Hill program via the Association of Baptists for World Evangelism (ABWE). City on a Hill is a program whereby American students will live in Thailand for seven months with their primary ministry being to teach English to Thai people. At the same time, missionaries from all over the region including India, China and the Philippines will then teach one and two week Bible discipleship modules to the American and Thai students.

"We may live the rest of our lives there," Lisa said. There was strong excitement and passion in their voices as they described the program and how they were going to make it happen. I told them they were sacrificing a lot to follow their path.

Rick brought up the missionaries he meets with when they return to visit the U.S. "Most of them say, 'I haven't given up anything, I've gotten back way more. We're doing exactly what we love to do.' If you love what you are doing, what have you given up? It's minimal. We're going to be in a new city of 11 million people. I wish we could go right now."

As I sat there, I couldn't help but marvel at their confidence. And I had to question it. I asked the one question we all wish we could answer, "How do you really know this is what you are supposed to do?"

They smiled. Lisa started, "We've asked that question a lot too. There is a passage in the book of Jeremiah that reads, 'If you seek me, you will find me. If you seek me with all of your heart, I will be by you.' At the same time, a person can say all of these things, but like climbing a mountain, it's not easy. Every step is hard and you don't know what is at the top. In the darkness, God is a lamp to your feet and light to your path."

Rick touched her knee caringly and looked at me. "This is not something you figure out with quick answers. Everyone thinks and operates differently. Seek God with the goal of being intimate with Him. Ask Him to make it clear. Then you have to start questioning. Are there events that have come into my life, are there people God has brought into my life to take me in a certain direction? Again, what is it that is in my heart that I really love to do?"

He then paused and took a breath. "Let me tell you how we've confirmed it in our hearts and minds:

"Number one is we have a desire. That desire has to come from somewhere. We can't discount that and say it's just emotion or just a feeling. You have to be careful to be sure it's not just emotional. We've asked and answered that.

"Number two, we've looked at the talents and abilities that God has given us to work with people, and primarily to work with students— talents to do exactly what we want to do.

"Number three, we see a lot of markers leading up to this.

"Four, we've gone to the Bible. It is clear in the scripture. 'Go to all of the world and preach His message.' We know we're supposed to do this. The question is where, when and how."

Then he added a fifth. "And we've gone back to our church, to people I've worked with and served under and asked, 'Do you see the necessary qualities and traits in us?' We've gotten confirmation. However, had they responded to us no, we don't see it, we would not have done it."

We talked for a few minutes more about the program. As we ended, I wished them luck and they gave me a hug. "There is no question in our minds."

At the time of this writing, Rick, Lisa, Kristin, and Ricky are in Thailand running the City on a Hill program.

REWIND

- My time with Rick and Lisa taught me a lot about decision making. Most big decisions have risk, but asking questions and then doing the research to affirm our answers will provide the same courage and conviction as Rick and Lisa.

  At the time I didn't realize it, but I followed Rick and Lisa's five confirmation points leading up to my decision to go on the road. These points can assist you with a lot of career decisions:

    1. You have the desire for a reason.

    2. You have unique talents and abilities. As Lisa said, "Don't take what you've been given and bury it."

    3. You have work and life experiences that seem to point you in a direction. What are your markers?

    4. You are driven by something besides money.

    5. You've sought advice and input from people you trust. And they affirmed your desire, talents and abilities.

- Many interviewees shared the power of their faith and spirituality with me. As I write this, I realize faith and spirituality are not universal. Some people believe in certain things and live in certain ways. Others don't. At the time of this writing, I am navigating my own spiritual road – acknowledging that it is there, but I am figuring out my faith and what it means to me.

  My time on the road has brought me into contact with a lot of people from a lot of different backgrounds. What I have seen is that faith and spirituality help provide many people with purpose. It provides some helpful guidelines for what they believe and how they should behave. At the core, whether you are Christian, Jew, Muslim, Buddhist, Hindu, Baha'i or practice any other religion, I have seen and felt that being in touch with your faith and spirituality can help you to get closer to your purpose and passion.

LESSON FIVE

Travel Your Own Road

I was one of the millions of people who listened to what society thought I should do for a career. I followed the money and tried to emulate someone else's career choices. When I entered the working world, I didn't have a direction. So I looked at my older brother's job in the sales field. He made a ton of money, worked minimal hours and got to take people (including me) to sporting events, lunches, dinners and golfing. Since I didn't know what I wanted do, I followed him into sales. And it was great, for a time.

Since then, I've learned that you can't cut and paste other people's careers into your own. What works for you is different from what works for someone else. I realize you are looking for guidance from this book, which details a lot of different people and their careers. The goal of the book is to share stories so that you can be inspired, educated and influenced. You will glean different things from different stories. One may speak to your personality, experience or present situation. But, you must realize that no two individuals—not even identical twins—have fingerprints that are exactly alike.

The same goes for careers. What worked for my brother did not work for me. What worked for my dad did not work for me. Our career fingerprints are uniquely our own.

As you travel the career road, you will be influenced by other people and by society's ideals. Your parents may pressure you to go into their field or a field they think fits you. Your friends may try to guide you down a specific path. A guidance counselor may offer words of wisdom. And society may influence what you do (or don't do). From what you've learned from the previous four lessons, you know that you want to get as much input, advice and guidance as you can. But, in the end, you are the driver.

We all will be faced with choices that I call "personal forks." These personal forks in the road can apply to all aspects of life: career, religion, dating, friends, purchases, etc. One fork is doing what we want to do (internally motivated). The other fork is doing what we think we are "supposed" to do (externally motivated). A big personal fork in my life was deciding between what I wanted to do (quit my job and cash in my savings to travel the country interviewing people) versus what I was supposed to do (stay at my job, get paid, move to the suburbs...).

There are a few things that we can allow to influence us at our personal forks. One is money. In Chapter Three, Terri Wardlow said she initially didn't follow her dream of being an educator because they didn't make enough money. The external factors won out over the internal. Yet, later in life, the internal motivation was still strong. Terri reversed course and now loves her job as a teacher and guidance counselor.

Two other influencers are social status and stigmas. We carry these into many decisions, including careers. As a career example, there is a stereotype attached to being a construction worker. There is also a stereotype attached with being an architect. On a business card, most of us would rather it read, Architect. Why, because it may sound "cooler" or appear to be successful? Yet in reality, construction workers can love the hands-on work they do (while making plenty of money doing it). They may even use as much problem-solving ability in transforming plans into reality. And some architects may wish they were alongside the construction worker doing the work, rather than being stuck in an office drawing blueprints.

What it comes down to is that many of us are influenced by the external more than the internal. We do that because that is what we've been taught. Society has showed us that we need nice things to be happy. It's been ingrained in us since we were kids. As a young child, you don't understand the difference between brand names. You don't know what is cool and what is not. You are just happy with what you have.

But at some point, we "grow up" and learn what our peers and neighbors value. Someone picks on us about where we live or what we are driving, wearing or doing. We see an advertisement, MTV Cribs, E! or a celebrity. We pine for a bigger house or a nicer car. And we change. We become self-conscious. We care about what others think. We try to keep up with the Joneses. And we say, "This isn't good enough anymore;

I need that." We have caught the social disease of conspicuous consumption.

I understand better than most how society can influence the way we think and act. My master's degree is in advertising. This multi-billion-dollar industry has been designed to convince us that if we have certain brands or products, we will be happier. And that clothes bought at Kmart or the inability to afford to take the family to Disney World should make us feel ashamed.

In America, our marketing and advertising is second to none. This means that since we've been children, we've been taught to think that a nice house, a nice car and nice clothes are the secrets to happiness. A rap song from my youth comes to mind when I think of this. It is by the Wu-Tang Clan and is titled, "C.R.E.A.M." (Cash Rules Everything Around Me). I've had those things. They are nice; but they are fleeting.

The point of this is not to say that money is bad. We need it to survive. But the lesson is that how you earn your money is more important than how much you earn.

For an extreme example, where the options are in greater contrast, let's look at a slum neighborhood. On one hand, there are people who value money over anything. They get their neighbors hooked on drugs. They steal and cheat their way to get the money they want. In the same ghetto, there are people who live hand to mouth working at low profile jobs that they may or may not love. These people live and breathe that how you make your money is more important than how much you make.

The former American Dream was to make as much money as you could no matter what you did. But many people have learned if you hate your job and get paid big time, you still aren't fulfilled (and your Ripple Effect could be detrimental to those around you). My vision of the American Dream is to determine what you are naturally good at and love to do, then get paid as much as possible for it!

To find the work that pays you both emotionally and financially, listen to the internal over the external. In the following chapters, you will learn about people who are traveling their own road. They are doing what they want to do, not what they think they are supposed to do.

CHAPTER TWELVE

Being Authentic Versus Obedient
When the dream job isn't what you thought

You can work very hard to try and funnel people into your life, but sometimes there is another power that decides for you. In one of my down times from being on the road, I called Rochester, New York's Advertising Council to see if I might get a local expert to look at a marketing proposal that I was working on. A few days later my phone rang and Brad VanAuken, who I had never met, said he was willing to talk with me.

Prior to our lunch meeting, I did some research on Brad. What I found shocked me. He had authored two books, *The Brand Management Checklist* and *Brand Aid*. One website reported he is, "recognized as one of the world's leading experts on brand management and marketing, Brad is a much sought after speaker, writer and consultant. He was formerly the director of brand management and marketing for Hallmark Cards, Inc."

Another website stated, "During his tenure, Hallmark market share increased by four points, Hallmark rose in the EquiTrend national quality brand ranking from 7th to 4th and Hallmark received the Brand Management of the Year award from Sales and Marketing Executives International. Brad graduated from Rensselaer Polytechnic Institute with a BS in Management and Harvard Business School with an MBA."

It turned out the guy who was willing to meet with a stranger for free to talk about a project he knew nothing about was a globally recognized branding expert. How cool is that?

Once I knew who Brad was, the lunch shifted from a time to talk about my marketing proposal to an interview about his career path.

We set up lunch at Hogan's Hideaway in Rochester. He strolled in, wearing a pair of khakis and a long-sleeved dress shirt, with the sleeves

rolled slightly. A wave of his hair in front bounced a bit as he walked. His cheerful smile instantly put me at ease.

Brad proceeded from small talk to discussing his education. "The best course I took at Harvard Business School was created based on the 'doing what you love' concept. It was called Self-Assessment and Career Development."

He described extensive journaling on various topics, such as: Go back to when you were a teenager, what was the coolest experience you remember? Go back to a time you hated, when you thought your life was falling apart and write about it. Go back to high school, what did you enjoy the most?

The course also used a lot of psychological instruments and vocational interest tests. They asked about possible role models: Who is your hero? Who do you most respect? Who did you learn the most from?

"The main theme was to pick out a series of things that really energized you and a series of things that enervated you. The concept was that if you could discover the things that motivate you and the things that don't motivate you, and overlay that to a job, you'd do exceedingly well. It was this whole sifting and self-exploration process. In the end, you came up with what they called, 'life themes.' These are things that really motivate you."

It sounded like a great class. If Harvard is teaching their students about passion, personality and motivation, why isn't everyone else?

He said Harvard spends a lot of money analyzing their alumni, trying to figure out what correlates to success and why some alumni were more successful than others. "What they discovered really differentiates people is that the ones who are doing what they love turn out to be the most successful because they really pour their heart and soul into it."

From Brad's self-assessment experiences, he determined a lot. He likes to achieve things. He thrives on variety, intellectual stimulation and working with other people. He said all of these were advantageous when working in a corporate environment. He decided that corporate culture was the important piece for his being happy at work. "I defined the culture I was looking for and figured out how I could find that."

After Harvard, Brad fielded a lot of job offers and chose Hallmark. He worked at their corporate headquarters in Kansas City, Missouri. "From the start, I loved the culture at Hallmark. I loved the creativity, the type of products and the type of people. It was a very creative, innovative environment." He mainly worked in entrepreneurial pockets of the company, where he could start and grow new businesses which were isolated from the core of Hallmark, the greeting cards.

Brad excelled at Hallmark and worked his way up the ranks. They pegged him as an up-and-comer and spent a lot of time and money grooming him for senior management. "They decided they didn't have enough leaders at the top, so they put me through all of these leadership development programs."

Hallmark paid for Brad to go to the Center for Creative Leadership, Personnel Decisions Inc., which is where they assign you a personal coach for a year, and sent him to a University of Kansas Executive Development Program. He also enrolled in numerous executive leadership courses.

His voice rose as he described creating new businesses for the various divisions of Hallmark. He loved creating and building new things and brands; at the same time he didn't have to be the figurehead. "I learned I am good at being the wizard, the person who comes up with the ideas and vision, someone who subtly influences. I'm like the advisor to the CEO. I'm like the puppeteer behind the puppet. And that's the role I like to play."

He continued, "I'm motivated by creating a different future. I envision a cool future for the world, for a city, for a place, for a company and then orchestrate everything behind the scenes to get us there."

He referenced a quote from former U.S. President Harry Truman, "It's amazing what you can get accomplished if you don't care who gets the credit."

Brad tried to apply that statement to his life. "The whole idea is if your ego isn't so caught up in taking credit for the change, you can make all these things happen and have the satisfaction of knowing you created the world you wanted to create. Powerful ideas have power. Someone else may jump on it and get the money out of it, but I've always been the person who really wanted to create the idea and the vision."

After more than ten years at Hallmark, Brad fulfilled one of his major career goals: he was the head of marketing for a large corporation. Yet, his vision of work and of himself began to change after he got his dream promotion. "When I was promoted to my position of heading brand management and marketing, all of a sudden I was in the core of the company, but I was also in the middle of a lot of politics."

His voice slowed and lowered in pitch. "It was like molasses to get anything through. Everything had to go through 10 committees—and this review committee and that review committee—it was very risk averse." The slow-moving pace did not fit his personality.

"I had been where everything was fast fast fast. Move; get things done; you've got to stay ahead of the competition. It was all about creating new ideas. Then I got into the core business, and it was all about looking the part, playing the part, playing the role, playing the politics and not really doing anything. I wasn't used to the molasses."

Even though he had achieved his career goal, inside Brad was struggling. "I didn't like my new role. At the same time, it was giving me great credentials, I was learning more, I was in the forefront of what was going on in the marketing industry and I was involved in a lot of benchmarking [benchmarking is establishing best practices in a field in order to give practitioners standards for which to strive against and which to compare their efforts]. But the bottom line is I started being out of sync."

It was a tough time for him. "Life was good. I had hit my goal. But, the problem was I felt like there was something inside of me dying because my creativity, my innovation, my entrepreneurial ability, anything that was expressing myself, it wasn't there."

Things were beginning to stray off the path so he sat down and did some self-assessment. He asked himself, "What are your goals for your personal life, your business life, your spiritual life, your economic life, your family life, your social life?"

Brad grew reflective as he spoke of that time. "I had done everything I had wanted to do. Everything I had ever wanted to be, it was already done. Now what?"

He looked back up and his voice rose. "An examined life is so important. So many people go through life robotically. They don't ask questions about what really makes them happy. Why am I operating the way I'm operating? Why am I here?"

Brad paused. "I've asked myself some very deep questions and my life has been much richer for it. You've got to create the life you want to create."

His eyes focused on me and he spoke in a tone that indicated I should pay attention; this next bit was going to be worth thinking over. "Society says achieve. Get more. More power. More money. Work harder. Sometimes you're asked to be obedient to things that make no sense. I question that. Rather than being obedient, be authentic. Be the person you were meant to be and follow the spirit within you."

And that's what Brad did. He followed his spirit and created the life he wanted. Brad gave up his dream job to start out on his own, feeding his entrepreneurial spirit as an author, speaker and consultant.

Brad smiled as he thought back. He held up three fingers and said, "There are three phases of my adult life.

"The first phase was doing what people expected of me. I went to all the right schools, I did well, I studied hard and I got good grades. I got the best job I could out of school. I was successful at Hallmark. Basically, I lived for somebody else and their vision.

"The second phase of my life was doing what I wanted to do." That was when he left Hallmark to go out on his own. "I had been doing everything based on what society says success should be and what my mother expected of me. At some point I broke away and said I like creativity. I like innovation. I'm more entrepreneurial. I'm really going to follow through on this Harvard Business School thing that says do what you love to do.

"The third phase is where I am now, in flow mode, where I've gotten in this really spiritual mode. I said I'm going to turn my life over to whatever you want to call it, to a higher power, and the power of the universe will direct me. It's a different level than I'm used to. You have to have the element of trust." He seemed to be very at peace with himself and the world.

He continued. "I don't have this big ego. I don't want to chase after the brass ring. I don't want to always feel bad because Bill Gates is still making more money than I am. There is always someone with more. I asked myself, 'When are you happiest?'

"My favorite thing is to walk through the back woods with my dogs. The sounds, the dogs sniffing around, the smell of the flowers. In truth, that's what makes me happy. I've already got that."

REWIND

Brad's journey can teach us on numerous topics:

- He shows us the importance of self-assessment. Once again, if Harvard is teaching their students self-assessment, there must be something to it.

  Go back to the section when Brad talks about his Harvard class, on page 84. Look at the questions he was asked and then answer them in your own words.

  Then go back to the introduction of Lesson Four, on page 60. Answer those questions. What do the answers tell you? Share your insights with someone close to you and get their feedback.

- Brad worked his way up and secured his dream job. Yet, it didn't turn out the way he had imagined. "The problem was I felt like there was something inside of me dying..." A key learning point is that Brad may have left his dream job, but he was still able to apply all of his knowledge, training and experiences to his new phase of life. He stayed in the same field, but created a different application for his skills, in a role he enjoyed more.

- Brad's insight about being authentic versus being obedient is one of my favorites. "Society says achieve. Get more. More power. More money. Work harder. Sometimes you're asked to be obedient to things that make no sense. I question that. Rather than being obedient, be authentic. Be the person you were meant to be and follow the spirit within you."

  Society says we should live in a certain way. This can cause us to do something just because that is what we are expected to do. Are you being obedient or authentic? What does the spirit within you want to do?

CHAPTER THIRTEEN

No Worries
Living in a shack with no roof or running water

For another exploration of what it means to live for internal versus external goals, I'd like to introduce you to Pete Campbell. Pete is a roofing shingler who marches to his own drum on the island of Martha's Vineyard. His story is less about career passion than it is about passion for location and lifestyle.

This chapter is more of a story than an interview. In fact, I never interviewed Pete about his work laying shingles on roofs around the island. I wasn't around during his work week. I hung out with him for one of the more unique weekends of my life; a summer weekend that showed me that it can take the influence of other people to help us break out of our comfort zones.

Having parked my SUV in Wood's Hole, I grabbed my bags and took the ferry over to Oak Bluffs. Pete was waiting for me at the dock wearing sunglasses and a big grin. He was about my height, dressed in a brown bowling shirt, a pair of low hanging shorts and sandals. His blonde hair was messy and spiked. "Hey Bro, welcome to the Vineyard," he said.

He threw one of my bags in the back of his beat-up grey truck. The truck was without a roof or a visible brand and rattled when he turned the key, but once we got going, it was good to go.

Pete's tan showcased his summer work. As he drove, he explained the layout of the island and where Billy Joel, the Kennedys and James Taylor, amongst other celebrities, had their huge houses. He drove me to the tourist spots and pointed out the multi-million dollar homes, some of which he had shingled. During the tour he explained that he enjoyed his work. He liked being outside and not having a boss looking over his shoulder. To me, what he described was not a true passion, yet he was very proud of how his shingling style was unique from most of the other craftsmen on the island.

NO WORRIES | 91

Eventually we headed back to drop off my stuff at his place, which he called "The Shack." We turned onto a dirt road and parked in front of a "mega-house," three stories with a two-level deck.

It was not The Shack.

We lugged my things down a trail into the woods and took a fork right. Ahead I saw a shed. I had been at Henry David Thoreau's Walden Pond the week before—The Shack was not much bigger than Thoreau's place. It was an A-frame, maybe 12 x 20 feet, without a fixed roof. It was covered by two blue tarps pulled taut and tied down in the corners.

"Welcome to The Shack," Pete said as he opened the door.

We were greeted warmly with the sounds of chirping by Stella, Pete's parakeet. She landed on his head as soon as we walked in. "This is home," he said as he put down my bags.

There was one couch on the back wall and another to my left. To my right, Pete's clothes hung from a makeshift open closet. A radio played jazz. Small storage compartments told me this may have been a workshop in the past. Pete's dirty clothes were in the front left corner. A box fan was humming and the windows were open. Pete had tie-dyed sheets and posters hanging on the ceiling. As I surveyed the room, he darted past the closet, up through a square hole and into a loft.

I looked up into the loft as Pete explained there was no running water, but that we had free reign of the mega-house. That alleviated some of my bathroom and shower anxieties. He also did his laundry and kept some groceries in the house.

I couldn't help but smile at my surroundings. Here I was in one of the wealthiest vacation spots in our country and I was living like a local, in The Shack. If you would have known me prior to going On the Road, you would have said there was no way I would've fit in at The Shack. I was not a camper or an outdoorsman. No roof and no running water? No way. Back then, I would've said, "Thanks, but no thanks," and headed to a hotel. But Pete's laidback, go-with-the-flow attitude intrigued me. I prepared myself for a weekend at The Shack and readied myself to live as Pete did.

Friday night was spent playing volleyball with some of his friends, throwing a feast at the mega-house and then enjoying an after-show-party at the house with a dance troupe in from New York City called the Rotate Dancers. The house was packed with fit, modelesque people. I hung out as long as I could, but at 3:30 a.m. I gave Pete the "let's go" look.

A low-hanging fog had settled in. I followed him down the dark, dirt path to The Shack. His bunk was in the loft area. He threw down a futon mattress and a sleeping bag for me. I did my best to get my contacts out with hands I had made sure to wash before we left the party. I brushed my teeth outside with water from my bottle. I thanked Pete for having me as his guest. "No worries, man," he said.

As I lay there, I laughed at the scene. I was going to sleep on the floor of The Shack. Laid-back-Pete and Stella were up in the loft talking. Earlier images of million dollar homes and swank hotels danced in my head, but I wanted no other experience than this one. The experience grew even more vivid as the creatures of the woods began to find me. A spider crawled on my sheet as I lay there. I killed it. Two ants marched by. I swiped them to the other side of the room. Some bugs buzzed by my ears. Normally that would've freaked me out, but Pete's chilled-out attitude must have bounced to me. I went out like a light on the floor of The Shack.

My alarm clock was the chirping of Stella mixed with the sounds of the awakening woods. I wasn't dreaming; I was still in The Shack. It was Saturday and I prepared for more fun.

Frisbee golf was enjoyable, until the fifth hole, when Pete told me to watch out for poison ivy. "It's everywhere," were his exact words. After golf we headed to South Beach. The sounds of the ocean mellowed me out. The hot sun felt wonderful on my back as I lay face down on my towel. Pete and I didn't say much to each other; we just enjoyed the day.

After an oceanside nap, a shower and some dinner, we went to see *Dance Martha Dance*, the performance by the Rotate Dancers. We sat in the front row next to the woman who owned the mega-house and a husband-and-wife team who Pete said created the Major League Baseball schedule each year.

After the show we went to a friend's house, a post-party at Tsunami, and then back to the mega-house for a post-post-party. At 4 a.m., I guided myself by the light of my cell phone down to The Shack. Stella and I greeted each other as I took out my contacts, brushed my teeth and lay down on the floor. I was awake long enough to marvel again at my circumstances. I had been traveling for months and this was the craziest place I had been. It was so different, yet so awesome.

At about 8:30 a.m. The Shack door opened and Pete sauntered in with a big grin. "Yo Bro!" He asked me to wake him up in a couple of hours and we'd go to Gayhead beach for my final day on the Vineyard.

Once Pete woke up, we drove to Gayhead. As we drove, he told me once you get away from the main beach entrance, Gayhead was clothing optional. This made me a bit uneasy. We entered through the main beach area and turned right. With the water on our left (and our swimsuits on), we walked away from the main crowd for about 15 minutes. The beach was incredibly beautiful. The waves crashed on huge boulders and the sand was coarse. To the right of the sand were huge bluffs, 50 feet high, with a kaleidoscope of colors swirling through the clay.

As we walked, I began to see people tan from head to toe strolling up and down the beach, as plain as day. Many were young, but many were not. There were some droopy butts, breasts and other parts. Some beachgoers had hats on. Some of them had fanny packs. Another had a belt on, I don't know why. Inwardly I laughed, but did not dare to smile.

I took pictures—of the eroding colors of the cliffs, not the naked people. As we walked, Pete told me about his Naked Phase, in San Francisco. I had never met someone who had experienced a Naked Phase.

Pete picked our chill spot, secluded up close to the cliffs. He finished his sandwich quickly and went to sleep. While I soaked up some sun, I got out my journal and jotted down notes about some of the people and activities. I was so glad to have made it to Martha's Vineyard. After a while, I stopped writing and looked around. No one was in sight. I glanced at Pete who was sound asleep. I began a chat with myself.

"I'm here, it's sunny out." I looked around and didn't see anyone coming. "What the hell."

Quietly, I took off my swimsuit, paused for a second and headed down toward the water. I was feeling carefree, but there was no way I was going to walk up and down the beach. "I'm naked," I laughed as I approached the water.

I hadn't had a Naked Phase, so my outdoor naked occasions up to that point took place at night in a warm pool, lake or ocean. That meant my butt hadn't seen the light of day since I was a baby. It must have illuminated the beach like a second sun. There were a few people down the way from me but I didn't pay any attention. I was naked. It felt incredibly liberating. I approached the surf.

It was freezing!

I felt like I was on a stage, so I couldn't just stand at the edge with my tiptoe in the water. I waded out and eventually crossed the line above the thigh. It was bitter cold! Yet, the wonderful feeling of the water enveloping me without clothes in the way returned in a rush. I waded out further, up to my neck, and floated. I looked back at the beach and the cliffs and Pete. I laughed again to myself. "How awesome is this? What an experience."

It didn't take long for the cold temperature of the water to overtake me and drive me back to the beach. I made a beeline for my towel, dried off and hurriedly pulled on my swimsuit. Pete was still asleep. I lay back down and smiled like I had just gotten away with doing something wrong. I felt mischievous but at the same time, invigorated. "I would have never done that in Charlotte," I thought. And I was positive of that.

As I left The Shack for the final time, I thanked Pete for letting me hang with him. He replied as he had often that weekend, "No worries, Bro."

REWIND

- This chapter is not really about Pete's career as a shingler. It is more about someone who has chosen the location and lifestyle of Martha's Vineyard as his passion. In one sense, he reminded me of myself back in Charlotte. He worked so he could play. After going on the road, I wasn't sure if I could just work to play anymore. But that doesn't mean other people can't be happy doing so.

- My time with Pete was a retreat that expanded my horizons. The whole weekend was about breaking down my perceived barriers. Before hanging with Pete, I would have freaked out at sleeping in a shack with no roof or running water, surrounded by bugs. I would have been uncomfortable roughing it. I would have kept my swimsuit on and been mad at myself later for not taking the risk.

- Pete marched to his own drum and lived by his own rules. His internal motivations were just different from mine. Pete showed me there are different ways of living and what works for one of us does not have to fit the rest of us. Oh, and I learned to not always take life so seriously! Slow down. Chill. "No worries, Bro."

CHAPTER FOURTEEN

Titles Are Irrelevant
From aerospace engineer to apartment maintenance man

One of the first questions we ask when meeting someone for the first time is, "So, what do you do?" The title that follows in the answer paints a picture. In a crowded room of strangers, if you had a choice between being an aerospace engineer or an apartment maintenance manager, which would you choose?

In Charlotte I worked from home, which allowed me to get to know the people who worked for my apartment complex. Whenever we'd have a maintenance issue, I would be on my computer or making phone calls when Paul Mapes, this happy-go-lucky, smiley guy would come over.

Paul would come in, quietly do his work and leave. We might talk a bit about the weather and the Panthers. I only knew Paul from a few meetings and a lot of hellos in passing, but from our conversations, I knew he wasn't the stereotypical maintenance guy.

My characterization of a maintenance man was a handy guy who might be a bit surly, with a beer belly and pants that fall off his butt when he bends down to fix something. He also might not be the sharpest tool in the shed.

But when I began my interviewing journey, I decided I wanted to talk to Paul because his demeanor was so relaxed and he always seemed to be so pleasant at work. It took some prodding and asking a few times, but Paul finally accepted. We sat down in my living room close to the end of my time in Charlotte. My roommate had already moved out, so we sat on some stray patio furniture.

Paul was in his late 30s, shorter than average, with dark hair and eyes. He had the opposite of a beer gut—he was very trim. When we spoke, he was dressed in his customary khakis, apartment logoed golf shirt and sneakers.

Paul did not speak with a southern twang so I knew he was like most of us in Charlotte—a northern transplant. He said he was born in a football town, Canton, Ohio, and moved to Pittsburgh when he was young. "I grew up loving Pitt football, but had to change sides when I started going to Penn State."

I didn't know he had gone to Penn State. My stereotypes about maintenance men reared their ugly heads when I assumed he did not graduate. "So how come you left school?" I asked.

I must not have been the first one to make that mistake; his expression didn't change and he didn't jump down my throat. "I started Penn State in chemical engineering and graduated in 1988."

I couldn't comprehend how he could be sitting there as a maintenance guy with a degree from Penn State, but I kept quiet. He said, matter-of-factly, "In college it was all theory theory theory. Penn State may not have been the best choice for me as an engineering school because they didn't have a lot of practical applications for the engineers at the school. It was mostly theory and it really turned me off. I ended up changing majors and going into aerospace engineering. It was possibly the hardest program in the school. As I said, I graduated in 1988."

Paul chose the engineering track after taking a personality test in high school. "It said I was very analytical and probably had the personality for an engineer." He followed that path, but his personality didn't quite fit. "I like being around people a lot. I like using my hands to fix things. I'm not really into theories." Still, he stuck it out for the aerospace degree.

After graduating, Paul moved to Florida and tried to get into the aerospace field, but timing was not on his side. The space shuttle had crashed not long before he moved. The job search did not go as planned. Meanwhile, his mother was working at an apartment community. She got him a job as a painter making decent money for someone right out of college.

Paul continued to talk, but I couldn't get over what he had said about graduating from Penn State. It took me aback. I even laughed out loud, not in a funny way, but in a 'holy crap you are shocking the hell out of me way.' I knew Paul well enough where I could laugh like that. I asked him, "Paul, so you're telling me you have a degree in aerospace engineering from Penn State, and you are here working in this apartment complex? Is this really what you want to do?"

He laughed. "Yeah, the degree was very hard to get. I think the mind and skills that you need for an engineer, you need for this. A lot of people in my field may not have the skills to become an engineer. They may have the analytical mind though." I could tell he felt proud for having that degree, but even prouder for doing what he likes to do.

"I like fixing things. The fixing part of me is being satisfied by this. The hands-on is great. I like the autonomy. I've worked in six or seven different communities and come across several thousand apartment dwellers from all walks of life. It's just me. That's all there is. I know if I fix it, it's going to be done right," he said smiling.

"I'm 38 and when I'm 60, I might not be doing this. But, I like a stable environment. I don't want to take a lot of risk with my job. Maintenance is pretty much never going to be outsourced like a lot of jobs today. They may bring in outside labor, but they're not going to outsource it to another country."

There was a pretty long pause. He looked directly at me. "People can trust me to come into their apartments when they are not there. You treat other people how you want to be treated. I enjoy making people happy. When I fix something for somebody and they let me know they appreciate it, I thrive on that."

Paul then talked about his wife and kids and the love he has for them. "She's my soulmate. I've been with her since I was 15. I knew she was the one for me. My family is my motivation. I like what I do, but if I had a choice, I'd rather be home with them. I come in here for what it gets my family."

We laughed at some of the stories he had. "Plunging toilets on a Saturday night is not fun. I don't get that too much anymore. I got smart and got everything running smoothly!"

His pager beeped and he said he had to leave shortly. I asked him if he wished he had gotten a job as an engineer. He thought about it for a second. "No. No. I have no interest in engineering. I am good at what I do. I don't need to make 100 grand a year. I know I don't ever want to work in a cubicle. I don't like being stuck in an office. I like being outside. I like variety."

And then he was out the door. I sat there in shock. My maintenance guy has an aerospace engineering degree from Penn State. Wow.

. . . .

REWIND

- Paul has found his niche where many with his educational background would not expect to find it. He has what we all want, purpose. He likes fixing things. He likes autonomy. He likes variety. He smiles while at work. And he is able to provide for his wife and two kids by doing things he enjoys.

- I'm not sure how many of us think we would choose to be a maintenance person over an aerospace engineer. The key is that it doesn't matter what the title on your business card reads, or even if you have one. It doesn't matter what others think. Paul is traveling his own road in the maintenance field. And life is good.

- I wonder what would have happened if Paul had found that coveted aerospace engineering job. Would he be wondering why he let himself get stuck in an office with nothing in his hands but a computer mouse?

CHAPTER FIFTEEN

You Get Out
What You Put In

When behind the scenes
makes the scene

There are millions of people who work under the radar. They are the people that help "successful" people get known and stay known. Meet Mary Ann Giglio, an anonymous superstar in the secretarial field. She is the assistant to George Fisher, the former chairman and CEO of Motorola, Inc. and Eastman Kodak Company.

Because Mary Ann is a close family friend, I knew she worked at the top of her profession. At the time of our talk, she was the executive assistant for George Fisher and formerly supported four previous Kodak CEOs. I was curious about her field and why she excelled. Our interview took place at Eastman Kodak Company's corporate headquarters in my hometown of Rochester, New York.

I stood in a hallway in front of a video camera, hit the intercom button, stated my name and heard a buzzer, indicating the office door was unlocked. I walked into the secure area. Mary Ann greeted me with a glowing smile and reached up to give me a hug (she is not even five feet tall). We sat at her desk, which was situated at the back corner of a large, windowless suite of rooms. George's office was to my left, but unfortunately, he was out of town.

Mary Ann had been running George's office since he joined Kodak in 1993. He retired from Kodak in December of 2000. "We're both retired. And he's paring down the number of boards he serves on," she chuckled. At the time of our interview he was fully occupied as the presiding director of General Motors and as a senior adviser for KKR, a private equity firm, and had just concluded his second term as chairman of the National Academy of Engineering. He sat on the Eli Lilly & Company board and was phasing out of the Delta Air lines board.

Mary Ann's path to becoming the office manager for a CEO of a global corporation started on her 14th birthday when her father bought her a typewriter. He did accounting for small businesses and with him standing over her; she typed W-2, IRS forms and other reports. "I had to be accurate. My dad worked in quality control and everything had to be precise. I knew what was expected, and that was my goal," she said with a laugh.

When Mary Ann was 17, Kodak was the premiere place to work in Rochester. Of the 350 students in her class at Nazareth Academy, she was

#1 in business. She also brought the added value of having studied two foreign languages, French and Italian. She was recruited by Kodak before graduation. As did all newly hired secretaries, Mary Ann began her career in the secretarial pool. After a few weeks, she was offered a permanent position in the international division. "I was very diligent about doing a good job, doing it well, doing it quickly and accurately. That was the standard Nazareth and my father had set."

The international group loved Mary Ann's work and they made sure that she stayed with them. Her experiences there exposed her to many new countries, ideas and international friendships. "It was like fertile ground. Kodak was really my formal education. I learned by working with very intelligent people who taught me a lot."

In the 1970s, the head of the European Region sent her to England, France and Germany so that she could personally meet her co-workers and see the different Kodak companies firsthand. "This was an unheard of opportunity for a secretary in those days. I eventually became the contact for all of the international VIPs when they attended meetings in Rochester. I was given that responsibility because one of my bosses said, 'I'm going to invest in you,'" she said with pride.

Working with various groups and divisions taught her a lot about herself and her field. "I was used to working unsupervised with the goal of getting all my work done. That means you must multitask, you have to use your intellect, you must be courteous, you have to be in control of yourself and not get stressed out in a very stressful environment. The most important responsibility you have is to always represent the office and the person that you work for in the best manner. I take that part of my job very seriously, but I do it joyfully."

A crossroads came for Mary Ann in her mid-thirties. While growing up, there were not many professional options for women: secretary, nurse or teacher. Twenty years later, other higher paying fields provided opportunities. Because of her skills and experience, Mary Ann was offered numerous jobs in other industries, but she chose to stay at Kodak. "I really liked what I did because I could make things happen. I was 32 and working for the COO of Kodak. I had a bird's eye view of what was going on in the entire company. It was a very exciting place to be. I didn't have a visible role, but I had a peer group of the top secretaries in Fortune 500 companies."

As we talked, the phone rang. The person on the other end had a schedule change for George. Mary Ann twice asked, "Are you sure?"

Once the answer was confirmed, Mary Ann sprang into action. The chain reaction that followed was based on one of George's philosophies: reducing cycle time (responsiveness). Mary Ann entered the appropriate changes in his Outlook calendar and synced it up with his office computer and PDA. A hard copy was printed out and put in the outgoing express mail folder so he would have it the next morning. A copy of the change was faxed somewhere. An email was sent and a voice mail left. All this occurred within a couple of minutes.

As the eyes and ears of four Kodak CEOs, Mary Ann had a lot of contact with the public. One story she told me with pride detailed a letter from a Rochester man who complained how dark the Kodak tower was at night. She agreed with him and brought his letter to George's attention. He assigned her the task of exploring the possibility of lighting the tower. She researched the costs, the means and the execution. When the project was finished, the man who wrote the letter was invited to switch on the lights. The tower lighting was covered by all the local news stations. "He gave such an eloquent speech about the power of the pen. Before, the Kodak sign appeared on only one side of the building. Now there was an identical sign on the opposite side and the tower was illuminated from the 16th floor all the way to the top of the roof. It has a wonderful effect."

We talked about the job of an executive assistant and the skills needed to excel. She described many communication and interpersonal skills as well as the ability to adapt to an ever-changing audience, even more important in a global society. You need creativity and balance, responsively fielding questions and solving problems while also dealing with always-changing details, meetings, travel arrangements, expense accounts and correspondence. "You have to be a reliable resource for your boss and for others."

She said the secretarial field is one without a lot of accolades. "If you expect recognition, which means you're doing it for a self-serving reason, this is not the field for you. This is the profession I chose and my job is to support people. It doesn't matter whether I am recognized or not. When I look at the Kodak tower all lit up, I know how it happened. When I look at the photographs taken of me with Meryl Streep or Muhammad Ali, I know why they were taken."

Mary Ann didn't say this in our interview, but because of our friendship, I also knew of some other experiences her job has afforded her. She's been personally thanked for her work by President George H.W. Bush when he visited Kodak in Rochester and she met President Jimmy Carter, the Queen of England while attending Royal Ascot, government officials in China as well as countless chairmen of Fortune 500 companies. Howard Bingham, Muhammad Ali's photographer, stops by her office when he is town. And she's been to the Olympics in Atlanta and Australia, twice attended the Rose Parade and Rose Bowl and walked the Red Carpet at the Academy Awards in Hollywood.

"They (the executives) should be in the limelight. If they have somebody competing with them for it, that doesn't work. To work behind the scene is my role. I prefer it. This is the way I want to work. If I can make my boss or Kodak look good, that is what matters to me. It's the greater good."

The form of recognition that makes her most proud took place when George Fisher first came to Kodak. Most new CEOs don't retain the previous CEOs assistant. However, four directors on the CEO search team recommended to George he keep Mary Ann as his assistant. And they've been an effective team ever since. She beamed, "Whatever you do lives beyond you. Your reputation is the only thing that you can't replace. If you always treat others as you'd like to be treated, it's simple. You don't even have to think about what you should do."

Mary Ann's rise to the top in her field can be attributed to having the opportunity to do what she is good at. "You've got to work at a job that gives you the liberty and ability to express your talents. When you do that, and those skills are desirable, then you are sought after. I'm good at organizing things. I'm really good at looking at something and figuring out how to set up a system. It seems that every place I've worked, I've reorganized it. And those systems have stayed in place even after I left."

We talked about secretarial careers. "It's a very exciting field. It gives you an opportunity to learn from many people and to interact with different types of personalities. It really gives you an opportunity to feel like you are contributing. It's a very important field because, like having a car without wheels, without secretaries you just can't go anywhere. You are not only the wheels, but you also provide the lubricant to make them turn easily."

We walked around her office and into George's. I held the Olympic Torch and Muhammad Ali's autographed boxing gloves. I asked her, "Did you ever imagine when you started that you'd be sitting in this office doing what you're doing?"

She laughed. "Never! I started out at 17. This was my college education. I have worked with individuals at every level in many parts of the world and no one would believe that this is where I got my education. I was chosen to work for top management because of my strong work ethic in the career path I took. You never know. I believe that God puts you where He wants you to be and gives you the talents and the opportunities to use them. I feel very blessed that He has given me these opportunities."

I came back to the recognition side of things. She worked with people making millions of dollars a year and I asked her if that ever bothered her. "It's been a very fulfilling career because I can see the results of what I do. There are higher paying jobs in other fields, but I found great satisfaction doing this type of work. Money couldn't buy the experiences I've had or the people I've met or the places I've been. If you need to be on stage instead of behind the scenes, this isn't a job for you. Although I've been behind the scenes, everybody has seen me through the curtains," she said with a gleam in her eye.

She paused for a moment and thought. "Your career is a big part of your life. It reflects who you are. You can't separate them. Choose a career that makes you feel good about yourself when you are doing it, one that you are excited about and that excitement stays with you. Just have this joy for life that comes from doing what you were created to do. We are each blessed with talents and you truly know what yours are when you enjoy using them. Only you know the secret; you have to unlock it."

As I left her office she gave me a big hug and said, "Work is like life. You get out what you put into it."

REWIND

- Mary Ann has put all of herself into her job. And she has excelled because of it. She had the talent, the drive and the opportunity. Her job has allowed her to see the world, receive an education from powerful people and utilize her skills to the fullest.

- This chapter speaks to all of the people behind the scenes. Many times we think the "well-known" person is the only one making things happen. In reality, it's the Mary Ann's of the world that allow the George Fisher's of the world to look good. "It's like having a car without wheels, you just can't go anywhere. You are not only the wheels, but you also provide the lubricant to make them turn easily."

Our culture tends to admire those who get media coverage, but that doesn't mean that is a value you have to live by. If having influence on outcomes is more important to you than visibility or credit (like Mary Ann and Brad VanAuken), then you may be happiest behind the scenes.

LESSON SIX

Opportunities Will Knock

In everyone's life, there will be moments that dictate the future. Mickey Weiser, the CEO of Weiser Security Services, my former employer, told me, "At some point, life hands everybody a break. The important thing is to take advantage of it. A relatively small percentage of people truly see the opportunity and decide to take advantage of it."

In some cases, we create our own opportunities. Examples of this are going to school to prepare for a career, working our way up for a promotion, going through training and certification for a profession or preparing over and over for an audition.

When you are prepared for an opportunity, it is an amazing thing. For me, the story that typifies being prepared is that of Chesley "Sully" Sullenberger. He was the pilot who safely landed US Airways flight 1549 with no functioning engines in the Hudson River on January 15, 2009, saving the lives of all 155 of his passengers. He went through the "routine" work of flying planes each day, but when it was time to overcome major obstacles, his training and preparedness paid off incredibly.

Yet, sometimes, we can get so focused on one opportunity that we are blind to others. Dante Jacuzzi's goal during his youth and the beginning of his career was to work for the family business, Jacuzzi (the international hot tub manufacturer). He quickly became the youngest VP in the history of the company. But when the family sold the business, his plan was upended. "My whole life had been focused on one thing. That was the only thing I knew. It was a big shock. All of a sudden I was trying to figure out what I was going to do for the rest of my life. What I had planned on doing for the rest of my life wasn't going to happen."

Dante ended up creating his own opportunities in various entrepreneurial endeavors.

I tried to learn from Dante's story. After I went on the road and realized my true passion was sharing the stories of passionate people, I spent over four years zeroed in on landing a book deal with a major New York City publisher. That was the only job that would make me happy. Still, I did keep my eyes slightly open to other opportunities. I became a public speaker, a professor at a college and joined forces with some innovation consultants. Then, after many nos and a few almost yeses, my agent and I finally went our separate ways without the book deal I coveted. I was devastated and confused, but in retrospect, it turned out that my road had widened over the course of time. Oh, and by the way; my book—this book—still got published!

So sometimes we create opportunities, sometimes they are serendipitous and sometimes they are forced on us. When Dante's family sold their business, he had opportunity forced on him. In the economic crisis of 2008, 2009 and 2010, opportunity was forced on millions of workers when they were told they were being let go/downsized/cut back. I know something about that feeling, as I was downsized from the second job of my earlier career. At that point, I was not fully aware of my own self-actualization needs, so I went out and got a similar job without reassessing what I wanted to do.

Whether you create your own chances or life presents a new fork in the road, an opportunity is an opportunity. The following chapters show four examples of people seizing opportunities, some created by their own hard work, some presented by happenstance and some forced on them in ways that did not initially come neatly labeled as "opportunity."

CHAPTER SIXTEEN

Overcoming Roadblocks
Seceding Key West, Florida from the United States

In our life we will all be given opportunities. But not every opportunity we get will be as unusual as Dennis Wardlow's. By answering the proverbial knock on his door, Dennis ended up creating a republic; the Conch Republic in Key West, Florida.

I arrived at Dennis' place in Marathon, Florida. He is five-three and trim. Even while inside, he kept his sunglasses on. He wore a lightweight, blue-collared shirt that was buttoned up to the middle of his tanned chest. A silver pen was clipped to his left, front pocket, coordinating with the shiny silver watch on his wrist. We exchanged small talk for a while and then delved into the topics of his hometown of Key West, politics and what he called "The Secession."

Dennis had a magnetic energy about him, laid back and intellectual. I must not have been the only one to feel it—he was the president of both his junior and senior high school classes in the early 1960s. After working in landscaping and electronic cabling, he entered the political arena in 1973 as a young upstart, defeating a long-time incumbent to become one of Key West's city commissioners.

Dennis is in the history books because of what happened on April 23, 1982. He was the mayor of Key West at the time when the city had a problem. This is the story of how Dennis solved that problem and became the Prime Minister of the Conch Republic.

As he began speaking, Dennis got a gleam in his eye and rocked back forth in his chair. A sly grin crossed his face. "It was a Sunday afternoon and I got a call from my dad who was a HAM radio operator. There was chatter about a roadblock in the Keys."

Dennis called the sheriff's department and the chief of police. They were also getting calls, but didn't know anything about a roadblock. "I went into the office on Monday and had a stack of phone calls from people who had been stuck in the roadblock. They were mad and wanted to know what the heck was going on."

There is only one driving route in and out of the Keys and the roadblock stopped traffic in both directions. "The roadblock was in Florida City, right when you get off the 18-mile stretch. You'll see the Last Chance Saloon. The

roadblock was right in front of their place. It caused a traffic jam 22 or 23 miles back. The officers said they were checking for illegal aliens."

Dennis started digging for answers. "I called our Representative in Tallahassee, a couple of the Senators, our people in Washington and no one knew anything about it. Then I called the border patrol, and they transferred me to the Captain. I introduced myself as the Mayor of Key West and told him we were getting calls from the chamber and numerous hotels and motels. I just wanted to know why they had set up this roadblock/checkpoint and what was going on."

He laughed. "The Captain said it was none of my business and that they were conducting a border check. I asked, 'How are you conducting a border check if we are a part of the United States? We're not a border!'"

The Captain said they were doing what they were doing and hung up. Although Dennis was tan, his face still got red at recalling the memory. "I guess at that point I made it my business."

Calls continued to pour in to the Mayor's office wanting to know what Dennis was going to do about the roadblock. He and some locals came together to discuss the situation. He met with John Magliola of the local radio station; Ed Swift, who was the owner of the Conch Train and Trolley; Townsend Kiefer, who wrote for the AP and UPI; and two other citizens. Again, the Mayor was asked what he was going to do.

Word was spreading in Miami and other places that you couldn't get in or out of Key West. Supply trucks didn't want to go south for their normal deliveries because of the roadblock. The roadblock was hurting the lifeblood of Key West—tourism.

Tuesday morning came and the Mayor worked with attorney Dave Horan. They ended up getting a date in federal court in Miami for Thursday at 9 a.m. "I went home that night and consulted with my wife. We'd always talked about the Conch Republic and maybe seceding. We always wanted to cut the bridges off. They're treating us like a foreign country, we ought to secede and become the Conch Republic. To hell with it.

"As she looked at me, it clicked," he said with a smile. I could tell Dennis enjoyed retelling the story.

The border patrol continued stopping cars and making a lot of people mad, especially the business owners of Key West. Dennis' phone continued to ring off the hook.

The night before their court date, the inner circle of locals floated the secession idea. Nothing was decided and on Thursday a group of five flew to Miami for the court appearance: The Mayor, Dave Horan, Virginia Panko from the hotel/motel association, Ed Swift and John Magliola.

The judge told Dennis he couldn't stop the roadblock, but that he would stop the traffic jam. The judge informed the border patrol that once the line got over ten cars, they had to let people through. At that point, the Captain unveiled his blueprints for a permanent roadblock. And there was not much Key West could do about it.

The Key West crew left the courtroom and were surrounded by a flock of reporters. Virginia Panko handed the Mayor the Key West flag. The mikes were shoved in Dennis' face. "Mr. Mayor, now that you can't stop the roadblocks, what are you going to do?"

The group looked at each other and at him. He leaned into the mikes, "Well, tomorrow at noon, in front of the chamber building, we will raise our flag and secede, becoming the Conch Republic." This set off a media frenzy. They got in their cars, sped off to the airport and flew back to Key West.

The group of rebels sprung into action. Townsend Keifer used his media contacts to spread the word about the secession. A secession speech was penned. They minted silver Conch Republic dollars with the conch shell and the flag.

At 6 a.m. on April 23, 1982 the Mayor got a call from the admiral at the Key West Navy base demanding to know what was going on. The secession story was plastered on the front page of the Miami Herald. The CIA, FBI and Secret Service were investigating to determine if they should arrest Dennis. He was also getting death threats.

Later that morning Dennis went to the chamber building in Founders Square. The silver Conch Republic dollars were given out to the reporters and bystanders. "The square was packed with TV cameras, reporters, people wearing business suits and people in shorts and sandals. I walked up to the platform with my wife, my son Joey and one of my detectives," he explained. His detective pushed Dennis' family aside because of the death threats.

Then the clock struck noon. Eyes across the country were on the Mayor of Key West, Florida. "They played the trumpets, I gave the signal to raise the flag and I started my succession speech. 'We hereby secede to become the Conch Republic...'" he said with a laugh. "We now declare war."

And with that, one of his policemen in a bi-plane dive bombed a Navy ship with ammunition of conch fritters, or "bollas." Two city commissioners in attendance "attacked" sailors and federal agents with stale Cuban bread. They hit a sailor over the head with the bread and were hitting bollas toward the ships.

"They ate all of our ammunition so we had to surrender," he howled. His laughter made me laugh. In order to rebuild the war-torn country, he asked for a billion dollars in foreign aid. "And from then on we became the Conch Republic. It's been an annual celebration ever since," he said with a grin.

The press ate it up. The Conch Republic had interviews on *Good Morning America, The Early Show, The Today Show* and in the international press. Dennis even got a call from his sister-in-law in San Diego because his picture was on the front page of her newspaper. "It was the biggest political publicity stunt that's ever been pulled.

No money involved. No consultants. No PR firms. There was nothing but us," he said proudly.

"We did it because there was a problem. It wasn't about self or profit. It was done because it was a way to say we are Americans and this is why we can protest. We don't burn flags. We don't roll in the middle of the streets. We don't become violent. It just worked out to be something that worked," he explained. The roadblock stayed there for two more weeks and it hasn't been seen or heard from since.

Dennis and his team helped put Key West on the map. The Conch Republic continues, serving to boost civic pride and sense of uniqueness, while also reaching out for trade and tourism. Cruise ships, navy vessels and the Coast Guard all fly the Conch Republic flag under the U.S. flag when they come into the harbor. The anniversary of the secession has turned into a big celebration and the Seven Mile Bridge Run is timed around it. Ministers and ambassadors of the Conch Republic are still being named, but Dennis Wardlow is the Prime Minister for life. He has stayed close to Key West since finishing his last stint in office in 1997.

We talked about how his experiences apply to life. He grew more serious. "It's tough out there, but everyone has an opportunity. At some point in time, a door opens. If you walk through it, it's an opportunity. If you stare at it, and wonder what if, what may be, it's never going to happen. If you worry about failure, you might as well grab a tent somewhere and sit in it because everybody is going to fail. Real failure is only if you don't try. Everybody is going to fail. If you tried to do a business and it didn't work and now you think 'I'm a failure.' No! If you fail, you learned something. You learned not to do it that way. You're a failure if you didn't try."

REWIND

- Dennis and his team had an opportunity forced on them by the border patrol and the courts. They had two choices. They could do nothing and remain silent. Or they could act to make a change. As he said, "At some point a door opens..." We know their results. Their door opened, they took a chance and walked through it to a history-making result. In the case of the Conch Republic, their need to make lemons into lemonade, and to find some opportunity in all the publicity, was apparent. A roadblock that causes a 22-mile logjam and economic harm is a pretty obvious, in-your-face call to action. The "Conchs" took action, but not everyone would have tackled the challenge with such innovation.

- In our personal careers, we may not see opportunities so clearly as calls to action. What if you get a job offer in a new city? What if a door opens with a start-up company or in a new field? What if you have a burning idea? I'm not saying to sprint through the door at every opportunity. The advice is to keep your eyes open and to not be afraid to take a chance. "Failure is only if you don't try."

- In cases where a career opportunity is forced on you (even when you don't want it to be) it is hard to see the opportunity. As I learned, it's never fun to be the one cut back, let go or downsized. Once the frustration and pain of being told goodbye is over, you have to look at it as a new fork in the road. Where will your opportunity come from? What doors do you want to open? What will you do to open doors for yourself?

CHAPTER SEVENTEEN

Are Loans Acceptable?

A great risk to make a great leap

I meet a lot of people who want to do something new. They talk about going back to school, starting a business, developing a product or shifting careers. Yet, many of them say they don't have the money to pursue their dream. This puts them at a crossroads. Some stay doing what they are doing. Others make a move with varying results. They begin their move by taking a second job, maxing out their credit cards or borrowing money.

I was in Asheville, North Carolina, when I had the chance to meet Brooke Priddy. The newspaper reporter who connected us told me Brooke was 27 and had just taken out loans to start her own dressmaking shop, Ship to Shore.

I pulled into a parking lot on Haywood Road and entered her boutique. Middle Eastern or Indian music played softly from the corner of the waiting area. Dresses were hung on three mannequins; one long and blue, one short and red, and one that looked to be a wedding gown. Brooke came out of the back office wearing a strapless powder blue dress that had a funky, crisscross pattern down the side of it. Her long red hair was pulled back, and some of it was in dreadlocks.

We sat in the middle of her design studio. As it turned out, Brooke and I were fellow road warriors. Her father worked for Phillip Morris and by age 16, she had moved 18 times. During elementary school, her mother sewed all of the clothes Brooke wore. "Once I became too cool for mom's dresses, I started making my own. I wanted everything I ever wore to be completely unique and one of a kind."

At the start, she would use already made dresses, break them apart and put them back together again in a new, unique way. The process evolved into taking some atypical fabric, not normally worn, such as drapery or

a Twister mat, and shaping it into something that she could wear. This got Brooke noticed. "People started asking me to make things for them. I started honing my skills and got better at it."

College also involved a lot of moving. She attended four different colleges, settling at the San Francisco Art Institute where she graduated in 2001 with an interdisciplinary fine arts degree that focused on sculpture and performance. After graduating, she and a friend took a celebratory road trip from San Francisco to New York City. I loved her free spirit. "When I got to New York and saw how much fun it was, I never went back to San Fran. I fell in love with the city and had all my stuff shipped to me," she laughed.

It was in New York City that her fashion passion took hold. Her friend was interning for Elisa Jimenez, a well respected fashion designer (of *Project Runway* fame). Brooke was able to sit in on meetings and volunteer backstage at fashion shows. "It inspired me," she said.

Life in Manhattan was not easy. Brooke had to work five jobs at galleries, bars and art schools to pay the bills. She would wear the dresses she made to work and people would ask her where she got them. That spurred Brooke on to make business cards so that when people would ask about her dresses, she'd set up a time to make them one of their own. "Every now and then I'd actually sell the work off my back. I would carry a change of clothes with me just in case. I loved doing it. I was making more money and having more fun making these clothes than I was at any of those five other jobs," she said. The seed was planted.

"I realized that nothing was as satisfying as making those clothes. I also realized it would be very hard for me to start my own business in New York." In 2002, family ties and the striking scenery brought Brooke to Wilmington, North Carolina where she started Ship to Shore out of the back room of an associate's boutique. The focus was not on individual dresses, but on creating a trademark bread-and-butter item via a line of bras and panties. With her goal to gain entry to boutiques across the country, she went on a unique sales blitz. "I made a little catalog and hit the road with a suitcase full of six different designs. Over three months I went to every major city on the east coast north of Georgia and south of Boston," she said.

The sales trip was not easy. She and her cocker spaniel stayed with friends, camped at State Parks and did what they could to eat. In each major city she averaged eight potential boutiques that fit her product line. Seven of them would say no. "They didn't like the idea of this crazy-looking girl coming in off the street with a suitcase full of bras and panties." Still, one boutique in each city said yes.

"It took a lot of getting shot down, and a lot of willpower to not just turn around and go home. At the beginning, I took it personally. I was getting down on my work, thinking I was not good enough. Every time I filled up the gas tank I questioned it." She ended up with 11 boutiques from the sales trip and broke even. But, it was hard to get reorders without being face to face.

"After that, I decided that maybe bras and panties were not the be all and end all. I wanted to get back to the things that were one of a kind, the dresses, because they were a lot more fun and inspiring. I got a lot out of the trip. A lot of the designs I have for Ship to Shore are designed by traveling and adventuring and searching for miracles. That's where I am at now," she said as she showed me different fabrics and the dresses she was working on.

In 2004, Brooke moved to Asheville to revamp Ship to Shore as her own dressmaking shop. "I had to have my own environment where I controlled the atmosphere and the sounds and the colors. I needed that. It's my nest," she said as she looked around.

Brooke may have had the goal of opening her own dress shop, but she didn't have the business skills or the money. She said a huge help to hitting her goal has been the small business classes she's been enrolled in for two years. "They helped me formulate a business plan, gauge potential costs and helped with organization and bookkeeping. Bookkeeping doesn't fit with my art school background," she laughed.

She opened her shop with small business loans. The pride Brooke took in her efforts emanated from her. She showed me several different dresses and told me about the people she's helped find the perfect dress. "I've found something I'm really good at. It makes me feel really wonderful to see someone walking gracefully down the street wearing something that I've made. It's the best feeling.

"The thing I really enjoy doing is meeting a woman who wants a dress for a special occasion, showing her the fabrics that I have here, letting her feel which one she likes the most, talking to her about her body type and how she feels about the way different things look on her. I'll draw some pictures for her, she'll choose what she likes and I'll make it for her. Interactive, one-of-a-kind designs, fit specifically for that person," she explained.

Her face lit up as she described a concert she went to a few days before. There was a girl dancing near the stage wearing a gown Brooke had made. "She was radiant. It wasn't just the dress, it was the whole entire image of her and her movements and the way she felt comfortable and the way her body was moving. It made me feel fantastic to see someone light up like that. That's enough for me. I'm just so proud. I feel the pride of my labor when I see it out there."

Being a small business owner, all of the creativity, productivity and financial work fall on her shoulders. "It's a big risk. I built this whole thing on loans. But, if I was still working until 2 a.m. at a bar, saving a little bit, I wouldn't be happy. I'll probably be paying it back until the day I die; but at least I'll be doing something I love.

"There is this line from a movie that runs through my heart all of the time, it's about finding your own path. The secret is finding something that you really love and doing it for the rest of your life. You just have to find it, which is trying everything until you find the thing you are really good at and really love, and then dive into it with all of your might."

We got up and she showed me some more of her work. There were four dresses in creation mode. There were also some bras and panties ready for packaging. Brooke smiled at me. "It takes a great risk to make a great leap. I've done it and I don't regret it."

• • • • • • • • • • • • • • • • •

REWIND

- Brooke created her own opportunity by having a plan. She enrolled in small business classes to balance her creativity with financial acumen. She took out loans to get started and sustained. Brooke's example shows that borrowing money to live your dream is risky, but can also be fulfilling. She could have chipped away by working numerous jobs and saving, but that didn't fit her do-it-now personality. If you have the vision, you have to gauge your risk tolerance and figure out a plan. On one hand, loans or financial backing have been key to a large percentage of successful entrepreneurial ventures. On the other hand, many people who have taken out loans have not been as successful as Brooke.

- It is also important to notice that Brooke's vision did not spring up overnight. She worked five jobs in New York City. She moved forward with what seemed like a practical scheme of catalog sales. She lived out of her car trying to sell her wares. After two years, she reassessed her plan and went into designing custom dresses. She changed cities. And she went into debt. But now, she is living her dream.

CHAPTER EIGHTEEN

Their Version of the American Dream

From the streets to the salon

In an unnamed city in the northeastern United States, I learned a story of drive and determination different from all the others I have heard. My meeting with two brothers from Vietnam took place as we drank beer and cooked steaks. For reasons you will learn about shortly, I could not use a tape recorder and cannot use the brothers' names.

I was taller in stature than they were, but their presence towered over me. They paced around the patio and ran their fingers through their long, dark hair as we talked. Tattoos dotted their forearms as they chain-smoked cigarettes.

Imagine being eight or ten years old and having your family tell you to pack your life into a bag. A war is coming. They tell you to say goodbye to your friends. Say goodbye to the grandmother who helped raise you. Say goodbye to your country. You do as you're told. You say your goodbyes.

Now it's time to sneak onto a boat with your family and a few strangers to try to escape to a place called America. A place you know little about. A place where they don't speak the same language as you do and has a different culture. You're not on a cruise ship; you're on a small boat captained by a guy who doesn't know where he is going. He's never been to America before. You cry and wonder what is happening.

My hosts are the younger generation of a family who escaped Vietnam before the fall of Saigon and made their way to the United States—the two brothers, their younger sister and their parents. The family could have chosen anywhere in the world, but their parents had heard about the land of opportunity, the land of freedom: The American Dream.

So they did what they had to do to come to America. The boat was cramped. People were sick. They traveled to Malaysia. After months of hiding, traveling and waiting, they finally arrived in the United States. That was the easy part.

Their parents had been told of a place in the southeastern U.S. and the family eventually settled there. So here you are in the Deep South. You don't speak any English, your parents speak very little English and you are told you must go to school. You are poor. There is not a private, Vietnamese school for you. There is not an English tutor. You go to class and people stare at you. What the teacher says makes no sense to you. She is like the teacher from the Charlie Brown cartoon; she speaks, but the sounds are not words, just sounds without meaning.

The parents shoot for the American Dream. They put in 80-hour weeks working at restaurants. They eventually open their own. They make enough money to buy a house and get you some clothes. But they are never home. They work. There are no vacations or weekends spent with them.

They are not there to walk you through your homework in this foreign language. They are not there to help you with your English. They can't take you to play sports or to friends' houses. They do their best to put food on the table and clothes on your back. Your parents are working 80 hours a week and are focused on their dream, which includes helping you financially. But you are left to grow up on your own. And it's not your parents fault—it's the American Dream.

Teachers don't take you in and try to help you speak or understand better. You are slowing them down. You are not learning in school. You don't understand what is taught, and therefore, you don't like it. You drift. Your parents aren't there to guide you in these uncharted waters. You drift further from school. You have friends who have similar backgrounds and experiences. Everyone feels the same thing. You drift together.

Now you are 16. School is a waste. Money is tight. You do the cooking and cleaning. Your clothes have holes. You decide you need to do something more with yourself. Your friends become your family. You are a gang. You learn from the streets. You protect yourself and your friends from others. You do what you can to make money. You take risks. Your group grows. Things happen. The group sees you as a leader. You start to think about your own American Dream.

Your parents are focused on making money. They work long hours but still struggle with bills. You do what you think you need to do. It's not always legal. You make money easier than your parents do. You make more money than they do. You help them with the bills. From all appearances, you're succeeding. Pride tells you to press on. You have a nice car. Girls want you. Guys respect you. Things are working out.

The years go on. You are the leaders. Then something happens. Something tells you that this might not be the way.

I am not sure what it was that happened—they wouldn't say—but the brothers split from the gang. I can't imagine it was easy to leave their lifestyle. Power. Cars. Women. Easy money. All without a formal education. But they left. They say there was no choice. They say not to use their names.

The oldest brother saw a way out. A way to make money. He saw it in the business that when you first meet him, you'd say does not match up: Nails.

If you get your nails done, think about who is doing them. More than likely it's someone from Vietnam. In the course of my interviews, I have heard a lot about passion and love for what you do. But not everyone has the same choices and opportunities. Look at the brothers' education and past. I'm not sure if they really know what they love to do. What they have is pride. They have such an immense pride in themselves that they will do whatever it takes to "make it." Their pride pushes them toward their own American Dream. So they both do nails.

They make enough money to live in nice houses, support themselves, their significant others, their children and their parents. But that is not the dream anymore. They are the second generation in America. They know what America has to offer and what it takes to get there. They want to see a better future for their kids. They want education for their kids.

The one way to that future is through money. That is what they want. That is what they value. Their dream is to own a nail shop.

They said they thank God for the nail business. It has been the way out for so many Vietnamese. This has been their path to the American Dream. They know what they know and their pride pushes them to work at their dream. Their dream will be fulfilled when they can walk into their own shops and see people doing the work that they used to do. When they can get out from behind the protective mask and leave the fumes behind. When they can shake the hands and say the hellos and watch the money flow into the cash register.

We spent most of that night outside under the stars talking, laughing and storytelling. I see their dream. They have the skills, the work ethic and the pride. They have already overcome so much, and because of that, they are already a success. I expect to see them succeed in their version of the American Dream.

· · · · · · · · · · · · · · · ·

REWIND

- Some people tell me they are stuck and that they have no options. The brothers show us that you may be drifting, you may have made some bad choices, or you may not have had as many opportunities as others, but you are never completely stuck. No matter when or where we are born, we all have dreams; it takes pride, purpose and passion to make them come true. Whatever your version of the American Dream, you can work your way towards it.

CHAPTER NINETEEN

Thanks for Your Hard Work and Dedication, but...

When your company cuts back

In the introduction to Lesson Six, I discussed how opportunities are sometimes forced upon us. This is definitely the case for those people who have been let go, cut back or downsized. These reductions in workforce have caused the psychological contract between an employee and employer to dissolve. Employees can no longer rely on working for the same company throughout their careers. And when the psychological contract gets broken, it leaves a scar.

The baby boomer generation (the 76 million people born in the U.S. from 1946 to 1964) has felt the impact of this deeper than most. Most of their parents went to work for a company and worked there until it was time to retire. Many of the baby boomers expected to follow the same path of one-company employment.

Over the course of my travels, I was connected to Carlos Hernandez, a baby boomer in San Francisco, California. He had similar one-company expectations for his career as a sales engineer at a Fortune 500 company in the electronics manufacturing industry. Yet, after 28 years of service, Carlos had a decision to make. His company was cutting back and was presenting scenarios for people (Carlos included) to leave their jobs immediately. They gave him five days to choose: leave now, or stick around with the chance you could be asked to leave later.

It was a gut-wrenching decision. "I was one of many people my age who thought I would retire from the company I started with. My father spent 45 years with his firm in a blue-collar role and I looked up to him as a role model of loyalty and stability. I had that vision for myself."

Carlos enjoyed his work and the things his success provided for him and his wife. "I was accustomed to the lifestyle of a company car, credit card and laptop. Personally, I was multi-tethered, like an octopus. More

importantly, my identity was really tethered to being an employee for a major corporation with a big brand name."

The cutbacks did not come as a complete shock to Carlos and he had done some previous analysis on what he would do if they tapped him. Yet, the reality that the cutbacks were directly hitting him hurt. "It was a loss. An emotional loss."

And change scared him. "I was used to one industry; the industry I was in. I was afraid of the job search. What would it be like to write a resume or go through interview stages? What would it be like to have new co-workers in a new office?"

Carlos' previous "what-if" analysis had somewhat prepared him for his crossroads. He knew the future at his company would be tough if he stayed. But Carlos used a golf analogy. He theorized, "I had spent all of this time on the practice range working on my driver, irons, pitches and putting. It was time to bring my work and personal life together. It was time to take it off the range and onto the course. The course called life. I had this inner thing going on: If I don't do it now, when?"

Carlos took one of the options and ventured out of a 28-year comfort zone. But he did not walk out of his company and into a new job. "It was a rude awakening for me."

The good news was that he was considered an expert in his industry. He worked with a recruiter and his former company's competitors wanted to talk with him. "That was very ego flattering.

"The bad news was that I was in a 'silo' (a focused skill set or industry). I was in a silo that contained my industry, my competitors and all the ancillary industries. Being in San Francisco, that silo was awfully old looking compared to social media and high-tech Silicon Valley. I asked myself if I wanted to stay in a silo where the size of the silo is continually shrinking." The answer was no.

Finding a new job in a different field in an economic slowdown was not easy. His recruiter was very blunt and told him, "Carlos, companies pay me a lot of money to fit into their glass slipper. And you are not it."

Carlos was stung. "I cried." In spite of his Stanford civil engineering degree and 28 successful years with a fortune 500 corporation, Carlos was not finding work.

He had been searching the usual job sites in his field, but once his recruiter smashed Carlos' potential glass slipper, his focus changed. "I saw that going down the traditional road was not the best use of my time."

Carlos went into action mode on the practice range. "I knew exactly the work that had to be done. At age 50, what I needed to understand was this whole thing about the web. In the process of learning about the web, I fell in love with social media. That is what was missing in my resume."

As Carlos learned more about social media and the current world of work, he saw a need: to help baby boomers use the power of the internet to help them in their career journey. Carlos' new career was to start a solo consulting company working with boomers either looking for work or looking to expand their personal brand through social media such as Delicious, Digg, Facebook, FriendFeed, LinkedIn, Meet-up, Skype, Twitter and WordPress.

"There is a fear of the exposure the internet brings. Life is now so public. The resume that used to be hidden with the HR manager is now on the internet for people to see and judge. In my work, I focus on how I overcame that fear so they can overcome that fear and gain a better chance of being hired. I also help them see how social media can help them overcome the invisible age discrimination that occurs for boomers."

He now works with people of varying ages who have been told "thanks, but no thanks" for their work. "It hurts emotionally. It is a process that needs to be dealt with. Give yourself time to grieve. Let it hurt. Let yourself be angry, and then heal. It's that same emotional loss I felt."

If you don't deal with the loss, it will fester. "It stays around and comes back to haunt you." Negativity or cynical thoughts might limit your job search or come out during a job interview.

Carlos tells those who are preparing for a change to take their current job title, go to a search engine, purposely choose an industry not your own, look at the jobs that are available and see where you are deficient. "That's what I did. It showed me where I needed to improve."

The second thing he tells people is to look back to 1492. "Why was Columbus hired to sail the ocean blue? To find an alternate trade route to the Far East. Everyone knew how to get to the Far East by going east of Europe. The Queen of Spain and Columbus took an alternate route." They were hoping to cut down on the length of time and high risk of the commonly used route.

"In careers, when will it be your time to take an alternate route?" Carlos asks. (And will that route lead to something far more interesting than your imagined goal, as did Spain's route west?)

After Carlos was cut back, he found inspiration from people who overcame the same obstacles he was facing. "Those people are the ones who modeled the process for me. They showed me that I'd be okay. The common things I have seen in them are: A. Attitude and B. Resiliency."

He says it helps to interact with people who have come out on the other side or are battling the same thing as you are. "Don't go about it alone. Find a support network. You can support each other. There are networking and peer groups you can join. You can attend conferences and get knowledge on what it takes financially, emotionally, professionally, etc."

By expanding your network, if the day comes when you are faced with change, "You're not floundering like a bird with one wing. At least you've done some homework. You can pick up the phone, call someone and ask, 'How did you do it?'"

Carlos also had the advantage of a coach. "She has been my coaching angel. She has meant so much to me emotionally in this process.

"A coach is good because they are neutral. Spouses can be too close to the scenario. The career shift rattles their cage around security and stability, and they are likely to be more emotional."

Carlos and his wife had been married for a year when his change of jobs took place. "We talked about it, but my leaving the company rather than sticking it out really unnerved her. It wasn't part of her plan for me and for us. It scared her."

Having a coach helped him navigate his way. "She is someone I can tell everything to. She listened and provided a safe place for me. I could be emotionally vulnerable and let her know how scared I was. As a man, that is a big deal. She knew how to give me baby steps and guide me to get from point A to point B."

And because the baby steps were steps forward, they were important. "You are not going to drive the ball from 180 to 280 overnight. If I get 10 yards and then 10 more, that makes a big difference."

Carlos took baby steps toward a new career, but also learned that life is different outside of the corporate cocoon. "Having to choose whether to stay or not showed me that no matter how stable things seem with a company, paychecks aren't guaranteed. My golf course changed. When you leave the so-called corporate stability, the stakes go up. The greens fees are higher, the course is tougher and there is more pressure to perform. I went from a casual municipal course all the way to the make-or-break PGA Tour. There is more pressure and more risk, but it always helps to have met people who have done it already and to know that they are okay."

He looked back on the timing of his job cut as a good thing. "This will sound weird, but it's true. I count my blessings that I had a head start and a runway compared to other people my age. It's strange; I left my company but my recruiter gave me the final push I needed. I'm not sure if I would have left the silo I was in without that awakening."

I asked Carlos to compare where he was prior to the cutback to where he is now. He pondered his answer for a moment and said, "If I had stayed, I would have let my self esteem be at the mercy of the company. Their acceptance would be allowing me to stay, yet they would hold the hammer. If I didn't meet certain performance standards or the company took a dip, I would be nailed. That is a high emotional price to pay."

He paused and then beamed. "I've had to make some lifestyle changes. I am making a lot less than I used to, but I am so much happier and more fulfilled. When I put in a good day's work, I feel so used up, but in a very good way. It is extremely satisfying."

REWIND

- Carlos was in a tough situation when his company cut back. He was used to the safety and paycheck that his 28 years in a Fortune 500 corporation provided. "I was multi-tethered, like an octopus." When the tethers were cut, he was forced to analyze his situation. Once outside the company, Carlos could see that he had been in a "silo" that was continually shrinking. He surveyed the situation, made a change, reinvented himself and now works in a job where he is happier and more fulfilled.

- Carlos shows that losing your job hurts, "It's an emotional loss." Through the support and inspiration of others, you can get through it. His coaching angel provided a safe place. He joined networking and peer groups. He attended conferences where people who lived through a cut back showed him he could do it too.

- Whether you are involved in a cut back, are looking for a new job or promotion, want to build your brand or want to pursue your passion, look back to 1492. What is your alternate route? What can you do differently than you've done before? What can you do differently (and better) than others? What makes you stand out as the Columbus of your field?

- Carlos was forced by his recruiter to face that his skill set was out of date and that he needed to retool. If you can do that kind of external scan before someone hits you over the head, you'll be more likely to grab an opportunity or overcome a setback.

- No matter what age you are, being part of a cut back is not an easy thing. It scars you. It makes you angry. It destroys the trust you have with an organization. But, after the sting of being let go subsides, eventually it becomes time to look at your new place in life as an opportunity, especially if the job you had was good for security, but not so good for purpose and passion.

Mary Wadhams, a career services expert told me, "For a lot of people it will take a bomb for them to get out of their job. We tend to hug the tree that we know, even if we don't necessarily like the tree we are hugging."

So in time, the cutback may not be such a bad thing. It hurts the pocketbook and scares us, but it also forces us to think about our career road. We are now free agents. We can ask: What is my passion? What is my purpose? What am I good at? What do I really want to do?

And then we can ask: What is my plan to get to where I want to go?

LESSON SEVEN

Don't Go It Alone

Previous lesson titles in this book say you are The One and you need to travel your own road, but this lesson qualifies that by saying you don't have to, and sometimes you can't, do it alone. In order to fulfill your dreams, you must have help along the way.

My journey typifies the help of others. There is no way I could have gone on the road without the moral support of my parents, family and friends. The journey would not have evolved into what it has become without the people who decided to share their stories with me. I am still amazed at the number of people who let me sleep on their couches, fed me, emailed me with good wishes or connected me to an interview. And once my time on the road slowed, my coach and mentors pushed me when the going got tough.

I have learned that other people can assist us, and, even better, that the peaks are sweeter and the valleys easier when we have a support group.

This lesson is twofold. The first chapter covers the importance of looking outside yourself for assistance through books, coaching and peer networks.

The second chapter focuses on the importance of family support. It covers an area I have not yet experienced myself; marriage and the support of a spouse. I've kept my ears open though, and learned from others. When I interviewed Glenn and Virginia Riffle, their life story was more about their relationship than about careers: they had been married for 53 years. They told me, "Married life is a 100/100, not 50/50. It's a give and take situation all the way. It's 100 per cent give on both parts."

When your family is a team, you can make decisions that benefit everyone, not just one family member. And when the peaks and valleys come, you will be able to handle it together.

The next two chapters will show you that the road does not have to be a lonely one.

CHAPTER TWENTY

Two Minds Are Better Than One

The importance of fellow travelers

In the previous chapter, Carlos Hernandez discussed his advice on ways to achieve your career goals. Part of what he said was, "Don't go about it alone." For him, that meant finding a career support network and utilizing a coach. He didn't rely solely on himself. In this chapter I will discuss what you can achieve when you allow yourself to get help from things such as books, coaching and peer groups.

When I moved back to my hometown of Rochester, New York, with the idea of writing a book about my interviews, Jennifer Sertl came into my life. She became my coach. She listened to my goals and vision. She got me to change some of my stubborn, sometimes nonsensical, predisposed ways of doing things. And she exposed me to new ideas and principles, in particular those found in two books: *Think and Grow Rich* by Napoleon Hill, and *As a Man Thinketh* by James Allen.

These two books have had a profound impact on my life. As I wrote this book, I wanted to go further into their teachings and sought out experts on each of the books. I was able to talk with Vic Johnson, an author and leader in the motivational speaking field who trumpets the book *As a Man Thinketh*, and Judy Williamson, the Director of the Napoleon Hill World Learning Center.

Both books reference the power of our minds and of positive thought, similar to the more recent book and movie, *The Secret*. I am going to write only tangentially about how to use your mind. You may wish to explore this area of inquiry on your own. Meanwhile, this chapter will help you reflect on how outside influences can help us get to where we want to go.

I spoke with Vic first, on the phone from his place in Melrose, Florida. His personal path led from being evicted from his home in his 40s to, within a few years, living his passions as a well-respected author and

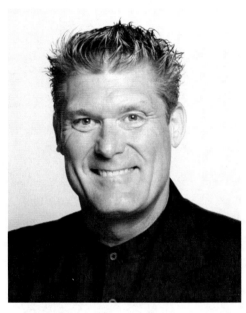

motivational speaker (he also became a millionaire in the process).

The kick-start to his growth came while attending a personal development seminar by Charlie "Tremendous" Jones. Vic explained, "Charlie told the group something that has always stuck with me. 'You are the same today as you'll be in five years except for two things: the books you read and the people you associate with.' If you have major changes in those two areas in your life, you are going to see major changes manifested in your life.

"The success I've had in the last 12 years has been totally due to those two things," Vic declared.

The first step for Vic was buying a bag of books the day of Charlie's seminar; a bag of books that included *As a Man Thinketh*. "That book radically altered my thinking and actions."

Then Vic created a habit of reading. "I was taught that if I took 15 minutes a day to read, at the end of the year I would have read six to 12 books. I became so enthralled that it grew to an hour a day and some days more. I would learn something new and then be able to put it into action and watch it work. Now, it's something I do unconsciously. I just do it. It's no different than brushing my teeth, putting my clothes on or combing my hair."

He has read over 1,000 books and cites his classics as *The Magic of Thinking Big*, by David Schwartz, *Think and Grow Rich* and *As a Man Thinketh*. "Once you begin to read as a habit, inside of a week, you will notice a change in the way you are thinking. You'll begin to see your world differently. No matter how bad things may be in your life at that time, it is all a matter of how you perceive it. That will create a hunger in you; a hunger for change and for more. In the process, you will seek out other people who are on a similar path."

This takes us to the second piece of the advice Vic received from "Tremendous" Jones, which is to think about the people you associate with. "If you are around people who don't have ambition and who talk constantly about how bad things are, chances are that is how you will also think. You'll see the same thing even if you don't want to feel that way. If you are around negativity, there is an influence on you as a result. You need to be with encouragers, people who are enthusiastic and lift you up. It is amazing how when you change your scene and get around people who are on a path of growth, the world looks totally different."

Vic says there are encouragers in every town and city in the world. You can find them through networking groups, friends, family members, co-workers or at Toastmasters, which is a group that meets and helps people become more comfortable speaking in front of an audience. "People who go there want to improve. They want to grow in some area of their life. They want to grow their self-confidence.

"When you begin to seek out groups like that, people and individuals will come into your life. There is a principle in the universe; whatever you are seeking is also seeking you. If you are seeking people of a like mind, they are also seeking you."

Then Vic offered the advice that fits my journey and this book to the core. "The primary principle I've employed for anything I've ever done is to find someone who has already done it and study what they did. Break it down to the smallest degree and study exactly the steps they took to be successful. And then, duplicate those steps. That's the shortest route to success."

He talked about studying people who are doing what you want to do, but also interacting with them. "Once you get around people who have done what you want to do and you talk with them, you begin to sense that they are ordinary people. They have done extraordinary things, but they are ordinary people. Then your own beliefs begin to change and grow. There is an osmosis that takes place, which is probably the biggest key there is to success.

"It's the belief that is instilled by being around someone who's done it and seeing the self-discipline that comes with it. It's the mindset of, 'Hey, I can do that.'"

Vic says we need to believe we can do it. "You've got to have a dream to have a dream come true. The reality is that many people give up too soon, too early. It is discouraging for me to see the potential that many people have who give up on their dream. They live with a quiet desperation. Benjamin Franklin wrote that most people die at 25 and we bury their bodies 40 years later. Living life without a dream has a huge, huge impact."

To get to where we want to go, Vic says we need to understand principles. "The Universe is not a respecter of individuals, it is a respecter of principles. If you employ the same principles as someone else does, you are going to get the same result. Gravity does not treat you differently than it treats me. It is a universal principle. The principles of success don't treat you any differently than they treat me. If I get very good at duplicating and picking the right people to duplicate, I have no way but to be successful."

In the early 1900's, Napoleon Hill spent 20 years interviewing, shadowing and learning from over 500 of the United States' most prominent people of wealth. Based on the lessons from these people, and at the height of the Great Depression in 1937, Hill released *Think and Grow Rich*. The book has since helped millions of people, including me, to focus on and achieve their dreams.

Because *Think and Grow Rich* had an impact on me (and because Hill passed away in 1970), I reached out to his foundation to learn more about how his experiences and teachings apply today. I was able to speak with Judy Williamson, the director of the Napoleon Hill World Learning Center in Hammond, Indiana.

She told me that before Hill died, he worked with W. Clement Stone on what became the 17 principles of success. The following four principles are the foundational cornerstones:

1. Definiteness of Purpose
2. Mastermind Alliance
3. Applied Faith
4. Going the Extra Mile

Because this chapter is about the impact of outside influences, I am going to focus on Principle 2, Mastermind Alliance. To Napoleon Hill, a Mastermind Alliance consists of two or more minds working actively together in perfect harmony toward a common definite objective.

In my eyes, this is your team. Judy expanded on this. "When likeminded people come together for a common purpose they can solve many problems, including their own, but also others that serve society."

When forming a Mastermind group, you need to start with the goals of the group. Ask: What it is that we want? Who could join our Mastermind Alliance to help us create that outcome? Judy said, "In a unified effort for a common good of the whole, everyone has the same drive and mission to make that happen."

Along with a common group goal, you need to insure that each person makes sure their personal goal is understood. "When the group originates and convenes, everyone needs to be paid for their services in some way. Payment can mean a lot of things besides money, such as recognition, achieving a personal goal, making an impact, etc. Each person may want something different, just as long as it is of equal value. That has to be agreed on before the group moves forward. Everyone should be compensated equally, but it doesn't mean compensated in the same manner."

When forming a Mastermind group, you don't want carbon copies of each other. "Don't pick people like yourself. Pick people who will expand your abilities. Interestingly, you do not have to like that person as a friend, but you still honor the skills they have and what they can bring to the group. Whoever is in your group must have characteristics, traits and abilities that you do not possess so that you are creating a well-rounded group."

You need to leverage your differences in order to maximize the impact of each person's strengths.

In the end, "A Mastermind group with affinity of thought will reach to a higher level, transcend their own abilities and have a way of infinite intelligence through their subconscious mind. This is a perfect harmony of individuals working together that transcends each individual mind."

We then shifted gears and I asked what Napoleon Hill would have thought about coaching. "To start, people in your Mastermind Alliance will coach you as you coach them. You need their traits just like they need yours."

Judy also echoed Vic's sentiments about interacting with others who are already a success or on a similar growth path. "In whatever field it is, you have to begin to associate with those who are doing it. Otherwise you are on the sidelines looking in. If you want to be an athlete, you have to play the sport. Just watching games and being a bystander is never going to create that opportunity for you."

Then she talked about Napoleon Hill. "He coached people to take ownership of their own lives. We are our individual self and we have to be able to grab hold of the reins of our life and lead it and guide it to where we want to go. This comes down to choices and self-discipline. We make daily choices and our choices begin to develop into our habits. And our habits, over time, create our destiny.

"To me, it is: Thought + Action = Success. Thought, even if it is the most pristine thought in the world, without action it is worthless. The least little action is worth more than the greatest thought.

"In *Think and Grow Rich*, Hill says, 'The secret is available in every page of this book.' Every single page talks about doing something. Doing it. Getting out there. Not talking about it and reading it. It's doing it. People who are successful are doers. Think as long as you need to, but then, once you've arrived at the decision, put that decision into action because that is what is going to create that outcome.

"For coaching, if you want to do something, look at the track record and map of others. It's not just a coach saying, 'You can become it.' You have to look at what the process is. Work with someone who has done what you want to do. If you have a specific area, it is hard for someone to create a roadmap for your success without having done it themselves.

"It's like school. You start with the general education courses, but once you know your major, you only take courses to get you to where you want to go."

In terms of coaching, I would summarize: if you don't know what you want to do, then a general career coach can help. But once you know your focus, then you should try to work with a more specific type of coach.

As we closed, Judy said, "Napoleon Hill believed that everyone has been put here with a mission already inside of them. Each of us is unique and in order to manifest who we are, our job as a person is to bring that mission into reality."

REWIND

- If, as Napoleon Hill said, "our job is to bring our mission into reality," then we need to do a few things in order to achieve that success. Contemplate the following items and how they may apply to you or to an alliance you have or could form.

  1. "You've got to have a dream to have a dream come true."
  2. "Grab hold of the reins of our lives."
  3. Thought + Action = Success
  4. "You are the same today as you'll be in five years except for two things: the books you read and the people you associate with."
  5. "Whatever you are seeking is also seeking you."
  6. "Get around people who have done what you want to do."
  7. "Get very good at duplicating and picking the right people to duplicate."
  8. Form a Mastermind Alliance "consisting of two or more minds working actively together in perfect harmony toward a common definite objective."
  9. Leverage your differences and maximize each other's strengths.
  10. You don't know it all. Allow yourself to be influenced.

CHAPTER TWENTY-ONE

Being a Team

When a wife finds her husband a job at a Las Vegas strip club

This second chapter of Lesson Seven examines the family dynamics that make up a career path. At a very basic level, life is easier if the two "significant others" are on the same team. Like the couple who had been married for 53 years, the Riffles, said in the lesson introduction, 100/100 works much better than 50/50. When the family is not a team, it can lead to anger, divorce and kids with mental scars.

All of us will face forks in the career road. These decisions are never easy. They get more complicated when you have a significant other. And are multiplied even more with kids.

What happens if one of us gets a job offer in a new city, do we take it? What if one of us can take a job making more money, but it requires extensive overnight travel, should we go for it? What if one of us hates our job and wants to do a career revamp? This could mean less money, financial risk or even new debt when starting a business or going back to school.

In thinking about these questions, it helps when the answers are a team decision. As you analyze questions, other questions will arise: What does this new career path mean to our relationship? How will it impact us? What will we have to sacrifice in order to attain our goals? Have we talked about this in detail and come up with a team decision? Do we both understand the relationship struggles that could come because of our decision? When the going gets tough, will we remember that we supported each other in the decision?

Once a team decision has been made, it is vital to support each other through the highs and lows. Career and life changes are not easy. There will be stress and pain. But the stress and pain will be reduced when you are on the road together. You need each other. I understand there are way too many factors to list, but at the core, the more you can support each other, the more of an asset you will be to one another. The more you argue and fight, the likelihood of success decreases.

When I look back on the advice I've been given about family and careers, these words come to mind: Trust is foundational. Mutual respect. Joint discussion. Joint decisions. Long-range thinking. Foresight. Team.

The next two questions should be asked once you know a relationship is long term, and then again once career forks present themselves: What do we value? What are our priorities? (Of course these questions should also be asked if you are single, but verbalizing them is even more vital in a relationship. In the ideal situation, a life partner encourages you to question yourself and verbalize your priorities, thereby gaining insight.)

Thinking about values and priorities should lead to some of these questions: Do we value work-life balance? Is it money? Is it time with each other? Is it time with family and friends? Is it church? Is it kids? Is it location? Is it...

The answers to what your values and priorities are will guide your way.

In the case of "Alec," he and his wife were guided by their priority to have a stay-at-home mom for their kids. They were able to build a unique career model on that priority because of their trust in each other.

I was in Las Vegas, Nevada, for a wedding and networked my way to a meeting with Alec, the manager of a strip club in town. The taxi driver told me I was going to one of the city's upper echelon clubs. He dropped me off and a mountain of a man greeted me at the door. I told him I was there to see Alec and he reached up to his shoulder mike and spoke into it. "Mountain" opened the door for me and an attractive young woman behind a cash register waved me through to the lobby.

A minute or so later a tall guy, maybe six-four, appearing to be in his late 30s with dark hair and a goatee strode through the curtains. He wore a fashionable suit and tie. Alec greeted me with a smile and a handshake. "C'mon in," he said as he pushed back the drapes that led me into the main dancing area. Montell Jordan sang to us, "This is how we do it..."

We went up a level, off to the left to an area where no one was sitting or dancing and sat down in two chairs positioned to give us a view of the entire club. We were right next to what looked like the VIP room. I looked down to the main stage at a tall, technologically enhanced blonde dancing. There was also another smaller stage to my right where a petite brunette danced.

Directly in front of me were the majority of the tables. Half were occupied by patrons, all guys. Approximately 15 dancers milled about, stopping to whisper things in the seated men's ears. Some of the girls would sit with them and some would move on. The bar was set back on a 45 degree angle to my right and there were a few girls sitting waiting for customers. I surveyed the view one more time before we began: I was surrounded by naked women.

The music was loud, so I had Alec clip on the mike for my tape recorder. He reaffirmed on tape that he would do the interview with the understanding that his and the club's identity would be kept confidential.

My preconceived notion of a strip club manager was a guy with a pocketful of drugs, shady in his dealings with the girls and the customers, and a guy you didn't want to mess with. Alec did not give off the vibe of a degenerate, he seemed peaceful. He explained that he had been in what he called the entertainment industry for just over 18 months, all of them at this club. Prior to managing the club he had owned a regional distribution trucking company for 17 years as well as a hair salon. "I had been in and out of the trucking industry three times. I sold the business and didn't have a direction."

His wife had family in Las Vegas and that is how they and their two kids, aged eight and nine at the time, ended up there.

His first job in Vegas was as a computer tech at a casino. It was a good job, but he wasn't happy doing it. "There was a lot of bureaucracy and a lot of paperwork at the casino. Coming from an entrepreneurial background, you want to do things in the most efficient manner. When you have bureaucracy layered on top of that, it is impossible. It was too structured for me after coming from owning my own business and being a consultant."

He left the casino and eventually came to work at the strip club. He started in security, then surveillance and was later promoted to working the back door. It was obvious that the club had a hierarchy just like any business. "As a prereq, you need to work the back door so you can spend time with the girls and let them get to know you. In order to work the floor you have to be very familiar with the young ladies. The back door is the way to meet everyone. It takes a while," he explained.

As a group of girls walked by, he pointed out one who was nice, one who was working her way through school and another who was trouble.

The next step up was floor host, which was a prized job because of the money it paid. "They don't just hire anybody off the street. You're dealing with people, alcohol and money. They want to be able to trust you and know that if things get out of hand, you won't lose your temper." It sounded like each level was a test… and I pictured many workers focusing more on the "eye candy" than on the job.

As a manager, Alec opens and runs the club with a staff of close to 100 people. Along with the dancers, cocktail waitresses, staff for two bars and shot girls, there was a DJ staff and a full kitchen covering from 4 p.m. to 6 a.m. There were also security people, office people upstairs, floor hosts, three managers in his position and house moms (who take care of the girls). He works five days a week from 10 to 12 hours each day, even more during the busy season. He was paid a salary, but makes most of his money from a tip pool shared by the hosts and managers.

Each girl is an independent contractor and Alec's experience with independent truckers and hair stylists prepared him well for the job. He likes this job because he gets to use his people skills. "It has a lot to do with my background. The thing I enjoy the most is trying to make things work. There are a lot more people problems as opposed to real operational problems here. It's amplified by the number of ladies, by alcohol and by the amount of money that's at stake."

Because of the money, a lot of his work is handling the girls' infighting. "The girls can make $200 a night and I've seen as much as $10,000."

It seemed to me he fit the entertainment business. "Being a former business owner, I enjoy the ability to make a difference in what's going on in the operations. In certain jobs you get frustrated because you don't have any power. In my case, I've had the power since I was 24. I'm 44 now and feel comfortable with the power. I can make a difference in terms of the experience the entertainers, the employees and the guests have. I take that seriously and it's satisfying to me."

The conversation paused and as I surveyed the scene, my eyes saw it all differently. This was a full-blown business, not just a party spot.

I was amazed to hear what he said next: "My wife got me this job."

I quizzed him at length. He explained, "She was a nurse and met one of the owners through the doctor's office where she worked. During conversation it came up that I was looking for a job. I interviewed with the owner five times and then started doing security."

I said it must be hard to fight the lure of the girls and for his wife to remain calm with his type of work. He didn't flinch. "My wife is obviously very comfortable with me being here or else I wouldn't have this job. She brought it to me. We talked about it. I don't have any jealousy to deal with from her. She's been in here, she knows what it's like and we go together to other clubs. I have a wonderful wife. That part of it, I have no trouble with."

I can tell when someone is telling me something because it will sound good on the tape. When he talked about his wife, my eyes and ears told me he was telling it like it is.

We then talked about his path in the trucking industry, at the hair salon and now at the strip club. "I love this job. I get paid to be nice to people. The worst part is the hours of the day I work. If I could take my job and move it to 8 to 5, that would make it the perfect job. I come in before 4 p.m. and get out at 2 or 3 a.m. With my kids it is tough. That is the worst part. But, my wife hasn't worked since I started here. It's nice she can spend time at home with them."

Alec and his wife discussed the strip club job at length prior to his interviewing and eventually accepting it. He wanted something new. They wanted her to stay at home with the kids. They talked about the pros and the cons. They knew what they were signing up for. Now she is a stay-at-home mom and he is a manager, working together to focus on their priorities.

REWIND

- In the Lesson Seven introduction, the Riffles told us that the secret to their 53 years of togetherness was, "Marriage is 100/100, not a 50/50." I did not expect to find an illustration of their advice via a strip club manager, but I did. Alec and his wife are living examples of a team that communicates and trusts each other. They decided on their priorities together, and together created a work life that fits their goals.

- Alec's story also shows us that stereotypes can mislead us. Walking in, I thought Alec would be a "grease ball," not a hardworking husband, father and former business owner. I saw his industry very narrowly. In actuality, Alec has applied his previous work experiences in an innovative way. He enjoys making things work, especially when people are involved. He enjoys making a difference in the operations of a company. And he enjoys his managerial power.

- Alec also shows that there are very few skill sets where the employment options are severely limited. Most industries and companies employ a broad range of workers, not just the ones we associate with that industry. If you want to be a stripper, your options are limited. If you are skilled at and enjoy a certain role, such as management, customer service, accounting, teaching or communications, there are many places to perform those functions beyond the stereotypes.

This also means if you have a broad education or career path, you may be able to narrow it down to a more focused niche and leverage those experiences. Here are a few examples that apply this idea:

    ◇ Teacher to industrial trainer, lawyer or politician
    ◇ Artist to package or graphic designer
    ◇ Fluency in a non-English language to translator
    ◇ Psychology to human resources
    ◇ Athletics to police or fire departments
    ◇ Travel to truck or taxi driver
    ◇ And yes, you can be like Alec and go from small business owner to strip club manager

LESSON EIGHT

To Change...

The biggest change decision I've dealt with in my life was leaving my sales job to travel the country interviewing people. Career changes are never easy because of the risk and the unknowable nature of the outcomes. There are so many factors that can, and in many cases should, influence our decisions. I won't list them all, but here are a few: purpose, passion, family, money, hours, benefits, location, corporate culture, boss, co-workers, training, capacity for stress, need for autonomy or structure, taking advantage of skills, building new skills and balance of work and personal life.

The hard part about careers is that we may not know if we like a job until we are doing it. Lee Hartman got the job he wanted out of college as a corrections officer, but he eventually learned it was not the right fit. "It wasn't what I thought it was going to be. It got to the point where I got sick to my stomach every morning when I got up for work," he said. Lee made a job change and is now happy as a Raleigh, North Carolina police officer.

I can't tell you to make a job change or not, but when the negative Ripple Effect of a wrong job choice creeps into you physically, it might be time to start looking for something new. The knowledge that you need to change jobs may not come to you overnight. It took me months of stress, contemplation, sleepless nights, grinding my teeth when I did sleep and trying various diversions or "escapes" before I finally made my career move. I went from, "What is wrong with me?" to, "I think I am going to do this," to, "I have to do this."

As human beings, we are predisposed to avoid change. In careers, that can cause us to stay in jobs longer than we want to or should. Remember what Mary Wadhams said in the rewind of Chapter 19. "For a lot of people it will take a bomb for them to get out of there. We tend to hug the tree that we know…"

The following three people have let go of that tree and forged new paths on their career road.

CHAPTER TWENTY-TWO

Keep Your Eyes
and Ears Open

There is more than one perfect job

On the road, I met a retired, high-ranking NASA employee who set up my interview with Dr. Mary Cleave, an astronaut he had worked with at NASA. Dr. Cleave had gone into space in the 1980s and was part of the Magellan project, which was the first planetary probe to be deployed from the Space Shuttle.

As part of my day in Washington, DC, I took in the sites of the Washington Monument, Lincoln Memorial, Reflecting Pool, Vietnam Memorial and World War II Memorial. Then I arrived at the NASA building on E Street.

Dr. Cleave was petite and I could immediately sense her intensity, as there was not much small talk. She had long hair with some grey streaks and wore small wire-framed glasses. I estimated that she was in her 50s. We sat in her large, corner office which was about the size of 10 or 12 office cubicles.

Dr. Cleave graduated from Colorado State with a bachelor's degree in biological sciences with an emphasis in botany. After graduation, she tried to use her interest in aviation to guide her career—she was in the flying club and had her pilot's license. "In 1969, women didn't become pilots, so I wanted to be an airline stewardess," she said. One problem: Dr. Cleave was five-two and you had to be five-four to be a stewardess.

With aviation out of the picture, she went to graduate school for microbial ecology, which is the relationship microorganisms have with one another and with their environment. Plants really intrigued her and she enjoyed thinking about how they interacted with the earth. "Lower plants are what make the world go round," she said.

After grad school, she came to a major fork in the road. Dr. Cleave was working as an engineer at a water lab, assessing the impacts of oil shale development on the Colorado River, but her long range plan was to get her Ph.D. in ecology. "When I was getting ready to go back to the ecology center, the engineers I was working for said, 'You don't want to be an ecologist; you want to be an environmental engineer.'"

She went back and forth on the career-change decision. She enjoyed the work as an engineer, but ecology was also very appealing. Her engineering co-workers saw something in her that she might not have seen. "The projects they were offering me out of the ecology center weren't anywhere close as interesting as working on the Colorado River, so I stayed on."

A few years later her co-workers once again saw something in her. "I was working at the Utah Water Research Lab as a research engineer. One of the other engineers was down at the local post office and up next to the 10 Most Wanted posters was a little sign saying NASA was looking for scientists and engineers to go work in space. He came back and said, 'Mary, you're the only engineer working here crazy enough,'" she laughed.

Dr. Cleave's face glowed as she told me how she got to NASA. She had been flying since she was 14 and had her pilot's license before her driver's license. "When I learned that part of the job was flying in T38s, all of a sudden I went, 'Wow, I can learn how to fly a high performance jet.' That sounded like it would be fun," she said.

In Chapter 11, missionary Rick Caynor talked about "markers." In this case, Dr. Cleave described a powerful déjà-vu feeling when things from the past came back to help her in the now. "All of a sudden I realized that without thinking about it, that I already did all the things needed to prepare for the job. Like scuba diving, flying and these seemingly unrelated things. You put the whole package together and say, 'Wow, was I thinking about that always?'" she said, grinning.

She grew up in the 1950s and 60s and laughed when I asked her if she was thinking about being an astronaut while growing up. "No. Because when I grew up, if I had said I wanted to be an astronaut my parents would've taken me to a child psychologist. They were all guys with crew cuts and jet jackets. Little girls weren't supposed to be like that."

There is a lot to be said for timing. "I hit affirmative action just right. I graduated in 1969. I was two inches too short to be an airline stewardess and 10 years later I was getting hired by NASA to train and become an astronaut. Big changes in 10 years."

She paused for a moment, then explained, "If you manage to get a ride in space, you are really just a fortunate person because it's such a privilege. Because so few people have done it."

My eyes darted to the pictures in her office taken from space. They were breathtaking. One in particular caught my eye; it was of the earth, except there were no borders, just colors. The picture was taken from the Magellan in the data-taking mode. "It measures all the plants on the planet every 48 hours. If you want to take global data consistently, that's a robotic mission, not a human space flight mission."

I quizzed her about her travels. "My first flight was in 1985 and the second was 1989. I've gone around the world in an hour and a half. I've crossed the United States in seven and a half minutes. You understand this is a really tiny place we live on. You get a feeling of infinity when you're down on the surface. When you get up out of it, you realize this is just a little chunk."

When I met Dr. Cleave, her role at NASA was doing advance planning for earth system science. She was gauging how the earth is changing and what it means for the environment. "We are trying to understand how what we are doing to the planet is impacting our life support system."

We talked about her findings. "We're getting warmer. Greenhouse gases are a large contributor to it. The fix is a hard sell when the traits you're talking about have really serious economic implications. The science is moving forward on climate change and modeling, but we need to bring along the economic models that allow our civilization to thrive in a non-petroleum-based civilization. It takes a whole bunch of people working together to make this happen."

I marveled at her career path and how she seemed to embrace change. She laughed. "Most people have a periodicity. You have to figure out what your periodicity is. For me, I'm a decade person. Every ten years or so, I need to do a total revamp on my work life or I get bored. Some people get bored a lot faster than me. Others, take a good research scientist, can spend their entire life concentrating on a little piece of physics and they don't ever feel like they need to leave that little piece. Everybody is a little different."

She talked about all of the analysis that comes with career changes. "If you really want to be happy you have to be less ego driven and more gut driven. That can be really difficult."

She explained how hard it was to deactivate her flying status to go to the Goddard Space Flight Center and work on robotic spacecraft. Her friends and family thought she was nuts. It was her periodicity.

"It's unfortunate that people seem to be overwhelmed with all the choices they have. They almost get lost in the choices. Given all the pressures you have around you, sometimes just finding the space to try and figure out what is really important to you helps."

I smiled. I had heard similar advice about finding time and space before. But coming from Dr. Cleave, the advice was different. Not all of us can be fortunate enough to find that time and space in outer space.

Being an astronaut and going into outer space gave Dr. Cleave a unique perspective on life and careers. She was able to see the earth as a tiny chunk. This helped her make more of her decisions with her gut, not her ego. I'm not advising you to book a trip into outer space so you can get a new perspective on things, but do what you can where you can to create reflective time and space. This could be as small as taking a walk or a trip to the park. Or you could plan more focused activities like a road trip or time at a retreat center.

I asked her to reflect back on her career road and how priorities have changed along the way. Her answer came more slowly than for previous topics. "Goals are great, but you need to leave your options open. Don't get trapped in them. You want to keep your eyes open because there may be something peripherally out there that's even better.

"Because that's what happened to me. I was going to be an ecologist; then I was going to be an environmental engineer. Everything was great and I was having a good time, when all of a sudden this little NASA ad was hung down at the Logan post office. And then I was an astronaut, and now I am in earth system science."

As I left her office, Dr. Cleave came back to a quote I share at all of my talks. "When you are thinking about careers or life, the best advice I can give is follow your gut, not your ego."

• • • • • • • • • • • • • • • • • • •

REWIND

- When I first set out on the road, I wanted to figure out the one perfect job for me. I know there are many other people out there searching for their own dream job. But Dr. Cleave shows us that it is allowable to do more than one thing and that we can be happy doing more than one thing. If your eyes and ears are open, opportunities will present themselves.

- Most of Dr. Cleave's opportunities were created by other people seeing things in her. Her co-workers recommended that she enter engineering. Another co-worker brought her the NASA ad. She was not dissatisfied by any of her jobs, but her eyes and ears were open to change. And she was able to go into space and then study the earth because of it. Have you tapped the wisdom of others in considering where you should go next?

- Next, think about your periodicity. Are you like Dr. Cleave and need to do a revamp every ten years? Or are you like a research scientist who can work on the same thing forever? Or is your time span much shorter? Knowing your periodicity may show you why you may be excited or dissatisfied by what you are doing.

- One of the biggest things you can take from this book is a deeper understanding of the constant battle that is being waged inside of us to try to "follow our gut, not our ego." In careers, you can think back to Paul Mapes who chose being an apartment maintenance man over being an aerospace engineer. Or Brad VanAuken, who left his dream job as head of marketing at Hallmark. Or Geoff Calkins' decision to leave a law firm to become a high school sports reporter.

In life, the gut versus ego fight is played out every day in our choices. It goes back to Lesson Five. Are we doing what we want to do (internally motivated)? Or, what others think we are "supposed" to do (externally motivated)?

When analyzing the gut and ego, listen to your values and priorities. Also remember what Brad VanAuken told us, "Be authentic, not obedient."

- What do you think would have happened had Mary Cleave been five-six and qualified to be a stewardess? Do you think that career would have satisfied her? Or, with her curiosity, talents and openness to change mixed with the help and suggestions of co-workers, might she have become one of the early female commercial pilots? Or ended up running Boeing's or Airbus' accident prevention or fuel conservation research departments? Might she have made it into space through another career route? Remember, "You want to keep your eyes open because there may be something peripherally out there that's even better!"

CHAPTER TWENTY-THREE

Self-Shock

When your plan changes

The process of making a career change is not easy. It causes us to ask a lot of questions that don't always have clear answers. In Rochester, New York, I met Fernan Cepero, who made a startling shift in his career road. At the time we met, he was the VP of Human Resources for all of Rochester's YMCAs as well as President of the Genesee Valley chapter of the Society for Human Resource Management (SHRM).

Fernan, 42, greeted me wearing a suit and led me to his office. He had dark curly hair and glasses. Placed around his desk and cabinet were artifacts from other countries. He also had some awards and a newspaper article that was written about his work at the YMCA hung up on the wall closest to the door.

Fernan's story did not begin on the traditional business path. "I actually started out wanting to be a curator in a museum," he explained. He went to school at Fordham University in the Bronx and double majored in Spanish and anthropology. He went on to grad school at American University in Washington, DC, and was working at The Smithsonian. "I was heading towards the career path I wanted."

He finished his master's degree and moved back to New York City and got a job interview with the American Museum of Natural History. "I figured this is it. Things are going according to plan," he said.

Fernan sailed through the intense interview process but was beginning to question if this was the field he wanted to work in. The job was doing research in a dusty, back-office basement of the museum with minimal interaction with others. The resources available to him would have been incredible, but something was missing. "I needed the people part. Something kept telling me, 'I don't want to do this. I really don't want to do this.' It baffled everybody. After going through almost seven years of schooling, this is what I wanted to do, what I thought was the job and career I'd want; but I came to the realization that I didn't want to do it, an awakening that, gosh, this isn't something I want to do.

"Before you even share it with anyone else, it's almost self-shock. I can't believe I am saying this to myself. I can't believe I don't want to do this. Part of me wanted to hold on to what I had learned. The big unanswered question for me was: 'What am I going to do with my degrees going forward?'

"Then came, 'How am I going to say this to my friends and family?' It's almost like you've done this awful thing and you feel like you're humbling yourself by telling everybody."

He declined the job and set out on a new path. "Surprisingly, when you do tell folks they are more supportive than you anticipate."

Fernan did his best to apply his education to the job search. "When I was applying for jobs, I was careful to pick and choose jobs that I thought would lend to utilizing the skill sets I had. My thought process at the time was, 'Because I have a background in cultural anthropology, let me pick multinational organizations that may need those skill sets at some point in time.' I kind of snuck myself into the workforce and then applied those skills."

His first job was at IBM in their international Americas/Far East division, handling their videoconference equipment for meetings. "That was an interesting position because I was dealing with, for that time, cutting-edge technology, and I was able to interact with counterparts in Japan and Australia. I could apply some of my awareness of anthropology and cultural differences to what their needs and wants were." He eventually rewrote equipment manuals so that non-technical people could understand them.

The IBM contract ended and he got a job at Xerox, holding various positions in billing, marketing, customer service and as a marketing manager. He was also doing work as an adjunct professor in anthropology.

Timing worked out well for Fernan. Because of his diverse experiences at Xerox and educational background, the company wanted him to work with their engineers. Xerox paid for him to get an engineering degree in structural design with a career track in human resources. "At that point they were really focusing on engineers and how to make them more productive and successful. Right around finishing my degree there were talks at the Engineering Excellence Institute about bringing in anthropologists to study these engineering groups to see how they worked and how to make them more productive."

This allowed Fernan to apply his anthropology knowledge. He worked with the engineering group, wrote a learning curriculum for engineers and eventually moved into the role of HR generalist, supporting the engineers he studied.

"What lent to my human resource success was the combination of having my education and working all of those years in various aspects of the business, like customer service, marketing, engineering and employee development. Although the path I took to HR was not a straight line, it all came together."

Fernan was at Xerox for 14 years and then came to the YMCA in his role as VP of Human Resources for the 15 branches in Rochester.

"I just did what I liked to do and what ended up happening was that I got paid to do what I like," he laughed.

Fernan talked about how much help he had from other people on his career road. "That was huge. Surround yourself with people who are going to support you and give you ideas and resources to help you achieve your goals and dreams. I am still in contact with those people who supported me. They said, 'We knew you would do it, we just weren't sure how you were going to get there.' You have to find unconditional support and steer yourself away from those who say you can't or you won't."

In his human resources position, Fernan sees a lot of people focused on the wrong things. "People don't really think about what makes them happy. They put all of their focus on money. You can't buy happiness," he said.

He went on to quote studies from SHRM that teach the same thing. If you dislike your job and they give you a raise, you may like it more for a week, a month or year; but eventually the money wears off and you are back to where you started, with a dislike for your job.

"You have to build your career to get to where you want to go. It's not going to just happen. Never lose that passion for what you know and for how you feel you need to apply it. It all counts. It's almost like starting your own small business. You are just trying to find your niche. That's really your goal. Once you find your niche and you find that you're happy doing that, you'll find the doors will open up."

Fernan's journey was not a standard line, but he was happy to have all of the experiences under his belt. "For the majority of us, there is a lot of soul searching and seeking until we find out what we want to do and until we find something we are truly happy doing. Every experience is a good experience."

The decision to leave a field, especially with years of education or experience, can be tough. "I never looked back with any regrets about why I did that. I am so glad I made the decision. I still use the knowledge and experiences. I don't know what the final outcome will be, but I'm really glad I made the decision."

REWIND

- Fernan talked about "self-shock" when he finally came to his career change decision. His focus had been set on a certain job. He spent seven years in school to prepare for the opportunity. But he passed on it and changed fields. He said it was a realization and an awakening.

If you are at a self-shock moment, think about what you can do to build your new career. If you have to start over or take a few steps back, the dues you may have to pay won't be as difficult if you have the passion for it. And be sure to do what Fernan did; surround yourself with a good team of supporters and allies.

- Anthropology is a niche field with a limited amount of funding and jobs. That makes Fernan's decision to turn down the research position at the American Museum of Natural History even more poignant.

It worked out because he figured out a way to blend his previous education and work experiences into his new career path. His years in school and at work were not wasted. As Fernan says, "I still use the knowledge and experiences."

We may not always see it, but there are ways to blend our past experiences into our current ones. Fernan shows us that if you are educated or trained and are attracted to a field that seems to be in a limited niche, you can apply your experience in nontraditional ways which can lead to creating a unique niche for yourself.

CHAPTER TWENTY-FOUR

Is This What I Want To Be Doing For 50 Years?

If you don't like it now, you probably won't like it later

In South Brunswick, New Jersey, I stayed at the home of Ginny Bowser and her son, Michael, who are my brother-in-law Bryan's mother and brother. Ginny set up my interview with a relatively new family doctor of osteopathic medicine, Hillary Beberman, D.O. I motored around an unfamiliar city following directions written on the back of an envelope. The turning lane roundabouts of New Jersey threw me off, but I made it to the next town over, Dayton, without incident.

When I arrived at the office, Dr. Beberman was with a patient. A few minutes later she came out of the examination room wearing the typical white medical coat with a stethoscope dangling from her neck. She was in her early 30s and slim with shoulder-length, brunette hair. Dr. Beberman welcomed me into her office and said that she found my interview search intriguing.

Her path did not start with medical school. Raised in Long Island, writing was her first interest. She worked as the editor of Brandeis University's paper and graduated in 1991 with a degree in American studies. Upon graduation, she took a well-paying job writing financial journals for Bloomberg in New York City. "It was fun, but really I wasn't that interested in it."

She liked the money, but eventually went through a phase of weighing her options. "Medicine was something that was on my mind. At Bloomberg, the pay was great and I was exposed to some great things, but I wasn't fulfilled. I asked myself, 'Is this what I want to be doing for 50 years? Am I helping people?' I wanted to make a difference. My parents were very idealistic and politically active in the 1960s. I was always brought up to want to make a difference. I didn't know if being a financial journalist let me feel like I was doing that," she explained.

She decided to apply to medical school and after taking some required courses, was accepted. "I said, 'If I don't do it now, I'll never do it. Let me try this. The worst that happens, I can always go back.' I had a long life ahead of me. I just went for it."

Then she grinned, "I left, but Bloomberg wasn't all bad. I did meet my husband there, so that was a bonus."

She started at the New York College of Osteopathic Medicine of the New York Institute. The difference hit her immediately. "In medical school I was very interested in the subject. It was the goal I really wanted."

The passion was there during medical school, but so were a lot of life changes outside of school. Dr. Beberman lost her younger sister to cancer, got married between her second and third years and had a baby during one residency. "Being a resident is brutal and I didn't know if this was for me. I had a lot going on and went through a period where I questioned it."

The time commitment was difficult and it was hard to leave her newborn. "You're working literally 30 hours at a stretch. You go home to sleep and you come back."

It was three years of incredibly long and exhausting shifts. The stress was compounded by the fact she had to work in areas of medicine she did not plan on going into, such as the emergency room and radiology. "There were times I was ready to quit. When I thought I couldn't take it. I missed my newborn son. 'It's not worth it. I hate this.' My friends were home with their babies. They had quit their jobs a long time ago. I said to myself, 'What am I doing? This is crazy.'"

But she pushed herself. "I almost quit, but this was my goal. I knew the pain was temporary and in 20 years I'd look back and ask why had I quit? Now I can say I'm so happy doing what I'm doing."

At the time of our interview Dr. Beberman had been out of medical school for two years and had been working at the family practice for a year, doing mostly internal medicine. Her schedule was flexible which was perfect for spending time with her two young kids. "I always wanted to be a mom too," she said as she showed me a picture of her children.

Helping people and making a difference was a theme that ran throughout a lot of the interviews. Dr. Beberman talked about how her job fills those needs. "Being a doctor you have to have that desire to help others because you deal with people all the time. You also have to be very patient. It's hard work. It's not the kind of job you go home and forget about until the next day. I'm always looking things up. It's a lifetime of constant learning."

Because her path had a few turns and bends, her advice for people struggling with their career choices built on her personal experience. "You have to think about what you really like to do. What do you want to do every day? Match a career where you can remotely do it. Even if you don't know, try something and then if you don't like it, switch and try something else. Try different things, because you will never really know if you like it until you are doing it."

Taking the final step of leaving a job is a major one, but she did it. "If there is something you are really unhappy doing, cut your losses. Like my job at Bloomberg, it was a good job, but if you're not happy, you've got to cut your losses. Residency was different because I knew it was temporary. If you don't like it now, you're probably not going to like it five years from now."

Losing her sister to cancer had a major impact on the way Dr. Beberman lived. "We were very close. After that, I decided that I have to enjoy life. You never know when something is going to happen. You really have to enjoy what you do. You need money to live and pay the mortgage, but it shouldn't be the driving force. You can't pick a profession based solely on that. You won't be happy. It's not worth it. In a way, it reaffirmed my decision to go into medicine."

She sighed and took a breath. I sensed she may have been thinking about her sister. After a second or two, she turned a little more upbeat as she told me about some of her patients and the bond she has with them. Her decision to leave the financial world and battle through residency feels worth it when her patients call to thank her for her work, bring her family cookies or they knit her kids a sweater.

It seemed like our conversation also reaffirmed her decision to go for her career in medicine. "I really feel satisfied with what I do. It's frustrating sometimes with managed care and insurance, but I really feel good. I know a lot of people don't feel like that. I can really say I am happy and I like what I do."

· · · · · · · · · · · · · · · · · · ·

REWIND

- Leaving a career for a new one is never simple. We may stick around in hopes things will improve. If external factors such as pay, your boss or a coworker are weighing you down, they may improve over time. If what you actually are doing for work is the issue, a quote from Dr. Beberman may be a foot on the gas pedal that some of us need. "If you don't like it now, you're probably not going to like it five years from now."

- Dr. Beberman said, "If you're not happy, you've got to cut your losses." She is not referring to a monetary type of loss. She is talking about a different kind of balance sheet. If you are analyzing your current state, take out a piece of paper. What are your assets in regards to your career? How do those assets impact your life? Does your career come up as a liability in regards to your personal fulfillment, stress, health and relationships? Make your list and then answer, what does your balance sheet of life look like?

LESSON NINE

Or Not To Change

In the course of this book you've read a lot of stories about people making career changes. Yet, it is equally vital to know that there are a lot of people who have always known what they've wanted to do, have done it, and are still happy doing it.

I do not fall into this category, but I am glad for those who do.

Basically, if you have had a passion for something for as long as you can remember, you won't want to make a career change. At the same time, just knowing what you want to do does not allow you to walk into your dream job. You still have to fight to get to where you want to go. Here are three stories of fighters who are living their passion.

CHAPTER TWENTY-FIVE

Marching To A Different Drum

A sense of wonder

The wonder is that we can see these trees and not wonder more.

~ Ralph Waldo Emerson

For over 150 years, my family has had a house on the beach of Lake Ontario in Rochester, New York. There is only one tree on our beach. It has watched over so many generations of our family. It may have even seen Native Americans canoeing along the lake before we arrived. So when the tree looked like it might be dying, I scoured the Yellow Pages for someone who could save our old family member.

Out of eleven pages of listings there was only one that didn't focus on tree removal. Dr. Daniel Marion and Associates' ad intrigued me. It said, "Tree Pathologist, Tree Preservation and Complete Treatment." The kicker was this line, "We Save Trees." I called and spoke with Dr. Dan Marion. He was an energetic sort and when I told him that another company wanted to cut down our tree, he got a nervous tone in his voice and said, "Before you do that, let's see what we can do to save that guy."

Dr. Marion came to the house and took root samples and scraped bark from a few spots. He thought they could save the tree with "systemic injections" and some other terms I didn't understand. After a summer's worth of working with "Dr. Dan," I knew his passion for trees was unmatched, and I felt drawn to get his story.

Our interview took place at the end of the summer. We rocked in two chairs on the patio with the waves of Lake Ontario lapping up on the shore 100 feet away.

It turns out Dr. Dan is one of approximately 15 practicing tree pathologists in the United States. This means he does laboratory

diagnostic work along with diagnostic field work, and then follows through on the actual treatment. His father was a forester and Dr. Dan's love for the outdoors was in him from the beginning. "I enjoyed studying nature, staring at nature as a young seven or eight-year-old. When I was outside playing and running around in my neighborhood, I was the one who would stand over an anthill and watch it for an hour. I really enjoyed staring at it and saying, 'Geez, I wonder why, how come, why is it doing that?' I wasn't just playing out in nature, I was wondering.

"I think that's one of the best things that a young person can do or say: 'I wonder if; I wonder why.' I think those are magic questions and magic words, 'I wonder.'"

A big laugh came from Dr. Dan as he recalled his early education. "I almost flunked out of fifth grade because my head was always out the window. I marched to the beat of a different drum from the beginning and why that is, I haven't got a clue."

His head was out the window in high school too. "My interest in the outdoors and my interest in studying living things caused me to be a big hack-around. I was a big screw-up in high school. But, I had a wonderful time and enjoyed biology so much they put me in the accelerated biology classes. It was the only class I was getting 97s and 98s."

Dr. Dan and his father would walk in the woods looking at trees. During one walk he asked his father why a group of tress was dying. He was told it was Dutch elm disease, a vascular fungus that killed groups of elm and maples, and that they didn't know how to control it. "When he told me there was nothing we could do, I couldn't accept it. 'It can't be this way. There has to be a way.'"

His love of trees led Dr. Dan to the University of Georgia where he double majored in Plant Pathology and Botany. Plant pathology is plant health and plant medicine. He went on for a master's in Environmental Biology Plant Pathology at Ohio University and then a Ph.D. in Plant Pathology at the University of Rhode Island. "I knew what I wanted the entire way through. I wanted to know the things that really had an impact on the health of trees."

The timing for his schooling at Rhode Island was perfect because he had the chance to study and work under some of the most recognized people in the tree pathology field. "Carl Beckman basically put vascular diseases on the map and researched how to deal with them. Nestor Caroselli was the original pioneer of systemic injections, like what we did for your tree. I was fortunate. There was no one else in the country at that time that had the expertise that they did. I took courses from them and they were on my thesis committee."

During his graduate schooling, Dr. Dan worked as a fungicide research and development specialist for a chemical company. His job was to take compounds that had promise for controlling certain plant health problems, set up research teams and evaluate the research with them. The goal was to develop the compounds and evaluate whether or not they worked.

As he worked on his doctorate, Dr. Dan ran the Disease and Diagnostic clinics for the state of Rhode Island. He also did work as a private researcher for industry, evaluating their chemicals and compounds and making recommendations to them on their effectiveness.

In 1974, Dr. Dan became a professor of tree and ornamental plant health at Finger Lakes Community College in Canandaigua, New York, and started his own tree pathology practice, Dr. Daniel Marion and Associates. He has been doing both ever since. "To this day, I wonder about a lot of things. When you say, 'I wonder if, I wonder what,' that helps mold your outlook on life. As we get older, we have a tendency to just put the blinders on. I have to do this. I'm going to go to work now. I've got to go buy this and be sure to change the oil every 3,000 miles. We just do what we need to survive in life. There is no 'I wonder' in that. We've kind of missed the boat as we've gone along in this country, in many countries. Most of us don't know how to stop and smell the roses."

A few years ago Dr. Dan made his first trip to the Redwood Forest and the giant sequoias in California. His face was joyful as he talked. "We rounded the corner and there was this huge, huge thing that's 20 feet in diameter. I said, 'Stop the car.' I got down on my knees and kissed the tree trunk. It was just such a beautiful thing. It was so gorgeous. I found a big rock, stretched out on it, looked straight up and stayed there for several hours, just watching. It was such a magnificent tree, 3,000 years old, a real beauty."

The redwoods enthralled him. He illustrated his description with gestures. "I have to get my hands on things. I patted the bark and 'Boom, boom, boom.' It was like hitting a bass drum. It finally came to me that the bark had to be two to three feet thick. That's its protection against fire. You get a lot of forest fires out there and it burns out a good amount of the bark, but very often it doesn't get down to the bottom of the bark and the tree survives. If it gets past the bark and to the wood, it will kill the tree."

He returned to the present. "All I knew was that I loved plants and trees. I wanted to be around them and I wanted to solve their problems. I could also see myself giving advice to people. Lo and behold, I became a professor giving advice to students. In my private practice, it's the same thing."

He stressed the need for intrinsic motives. "If you're working with living things whether it's trees, or animals or humans, there's got to be another reason why you want to be there. I know I wouldn't want to have a doctor working on me who was just interested in the money."

We talked about his work with students and people who choose their career path based solely on money. "I feel bad for those who can't wonder and think about what they really want to be or do or how they want to exist. If the reason you are going into a field is because it's a well-paying job, then you've missed your passion 100 per cent. You just totally slid past your whole life. Now you chase the money and do like everybody else, like the old adage of lemmings jumping off a cliff.

"As a first step, do not ask yourself about the money; don't even ask if a job exists in this field. If you like doing something, analyze how you can transform it into something where there is a need." And where there is a need, there is a market (and money).

"If you have fear and trepidation, close your eyes and keep them closed for half an hour and try to envision yourself doing whatever it is in this world that would make you the happiest; and that you might be able to get compensated for doing it. You have to be able to see yourself doing it and then you have to see yourself with a smile on your face.

"You have to ask yourself, how do I want to exist? There are a lot of things you can do, but what you choose has to give you fulfillment."

I told him he was lucky to have found the career he loved. He said it wasn't luck. "I tell my students it's the PDD: the persistence, the drive and the determination. We all fail, but you can't ever give up when you do. Failure is one of the best teachers there is. It makes you think back and wonder. If you're worried about money, find a niche. Find your passion, then find your skills, then find your niche. You'll be a little bug in a little crevice and any ant that comes along you can jump on them."

Dr. Dan found his niche in the tree and plant world. He now has five people working in his lab, he travels the world giving talks and is on the board of International Society of Arbor Culture. Our tree received Dr. Dan's total holistic health package of systemic injections for the roots and trunk as well as an increase in the host-pathogen ratio. The tree is thriving.

· · · · · · · · · · · · · · · · · ·
REWIND

- Dr. Dan knew what he wanted to do since he was in fifth grade. He is fueled by a sense of wonder and has never wanted to stray from his path. He shows that you can harness your passion, even if it is very narrow, and work in extraordinary ways. I am not sure how many of us have a desire to become a tree pathologist. What I do know is that we'd all like to be as passionate and energetic as Dr. Dan.

- If you know what your passion is, let your persistence, drive and determination carry you.

CHAPTER TWENTY-SIX

Paying Your Dues

A scene in the movie business

If you have never been to New York City, words will not do it justice. You have to feel the energy walking the sidewalks, riding the subways and in the restaurants and bars. You have to climb the Statue of Liberty, ride in a yellow taxi, stride down Wall Street, stroll across the Brooklyn Bridge and stand and reflect at Ground Zero. Take in the surreal natural wonder surrounded by cliffs of skyscrapers that is Central Park, the lights of Times Square, the Metropolitan Museum of Art, fisherman's wharf, Yankee Stadium, Madison Square Garden and the wide diversity of people, the cornucopia of cultures, accents and languages.

When I was in the Big Apple I had the chance to meet Mary Cameron ("M.C.") VanGraafeiland, a senior publicist for Warner Brothers studios. Our interview took place, interestingly enough, on the afternoon of the Oscars. "When I was growing up, watching the Oscars was such an event for me. No one could speak to me. I wouldn't take any phone calls. I had to concentrate and focus on it."

She grew up in Raleigh, North Carolina, with a love of performing; theater, dancing, music and the arts were always a big part of her life. Yet for a job, she didn't picture herself working as an actress. "I didn't think I had the fire to pursue performance as a career, but I also knew I still wanted to be a part of it."

M.C. enrolled at the University of North Carolina at Chapel Hill and studied journalism, with the goal of becoming an on-air reporter. After two years she learned that reporters had to, "move to Duluth and start out making 19 grand a year." That changed her mind. "I realized my passion for it wasn't as strong I thought it would've been. I realized I was more interested in the entertainment industry."

During her junior year she sent resumes for internships to Los Angeles and New York. She was "hired" at *The Late Show with David Letterman* as an unpaid intern. The job was in the talent department, whose main responsibility was booking the celebrity guests for the show. "Once I got up here and interned at Letterman, I said this is what I want to do. I knew it, I just didn't know exactly how."

After Letterman, M.C. returned to school and did an internship every semester beginning her junior year, including one at UNC-TV and one for the southeastern bureau head of NPR (National Public Radio). "I'm so thankful my parents encouraged me to do internships. I wish I had done tons more of them. You just learn so much by being out there and doing and seeing. You see the pros and cons. It's kind of like dating. You have to get out there and try it. Even if after every internship you try, you say, 'Never in a million years would I want to do this for a living,' at least you know that and can look at something else."

Upon graduation, M.C. had to decide between L.A. and New York. She called her old boss at Letterman, who suggested she take a job as a page at CBS. Some of the United States' most prominent journalists and entertainers started off as pages. M.C. did administrative jobs within numerous CBS departments. "It was almost like being a glorified intern. You got paid a little bit of money, but not a lot."

In the evenings most of the pages would go to Letterman and work in audience services, lining up the audience, getting them in the theater, seating them and then getting them out. Because of her previous experience at Letterman, M.C. ended up being placed there permanently, in the audience services department, recruiting the audience for the show. She was lucky; most pages don't get steady work or steady paychecks. "It was awesome. I got everyone I knew in to see the show. And once the show starts, the pages stand at the door to make sure no one goes in or out. I saw some amazing guests and incredible bands."

There was not a lot of room for growth at Letterman. After six months, M.C. wanted to widen her experience in order to become more marketable for whatever she decided was next. She left to take part in an executive training program at a mid-sized public relations firm, Ruder Finn. She was in the Planned Television Arts division. Their niche was setting authors up for a morning drive radio tour or a satellite television tour. "They gave me my own books to promote. They gave me a contact book with different stations and said, 'Call the morning show producers and pitch this book. Put together a tour.' I enjoyed the creativity that came with it."

While at Ruder Finn, M.C. got a call from Warner Brothers studios. They contacted her because of her experience working with talent at Letterman, together with her pitching experience at Ruder Finn. Warner Brothers was looking for a publicity coordinator for the magazine department. "I said this is it. This is what I want to do."

Starting as an assistant to the magazine publicist, M.C. helped pitch articles about Warner Brothers' movies to any and all magazines. As she got more experience and the division's workload increased, her boss gave M.C. work pitching stories to specific media outlets. "When *Harry Potter* came out, it was such an overwhelming film; she let me take the teen and kids' publications. I got to pitch *Teen People, Teen Vogue, TIME for Kids, Scholastic, Nickelodeon* and a lot of others. Because it was a fantasy type of project, it was easy to be creative and push the envelope."

After being coordinator for less than three years, M.C. was promoted to junior publicist within the magazine division. This meant she had her own campaigns. "In the print world, you really get to see the fruits of your labor. I loved that. There is something tangible. You can pick up the magazine, see the interview in print and see the photos that you sent them. You can see the photo shoot that you set up and how the photos turned out."

When Warner Brothers restructured their publicity departments, M.C. moved to the television side of things. She had been there for three years when, the week before our interview, she was promoted to senior publicist. She was pumped.

M.C.'s job doing television publicity will make some people jealous. She gets to rub elbows with the stars. Typically during the week before a movie opens, the stars will come to New York City for a media blitz. "There is always a Warner Brothers person with the talent when they are making these appearances. That can be kind of fun. They appear on various shows like *The Today Show, GMA, Letterman, Conan, The View* and *Regis and Kelly.*"

M.C. had some good stories about the fringe benefits of the job. She attended the National Board of Review movie awards, sitting in the Tavern on the Green at tables next to Clint Eastwood and Annette Benning. She worked closely with director Tim Burton on *Charlie and the Chocolate Factory* and *Corpse Bride.* Because of that, she flew with him and his team, at his request, on the private Warner Brothers jet for work in Los Angeles.

One of her favorite stories occurred during her work on *The Perfect Storm.* "I was assigned to George Clooney and his group of family and friends. It was nerve wracking and incredibly exciting. We had to go from Boston to Gloucester for the premiere. We had this whole fleet of cars. I had to get all of his people in the cars on time, set up security—we even had a police escort all the way there. It was crazy."

They did the red carpet premier, watched the film, went to the after-party and mingled with all of the townspeople. Clooney signed a lot of autographs and it got to be late. It was time to go and his assistant approached M.C. and told her that she was coming with them.

M.C. smiled as she told the story. "It was really late and we went back to the Ritz in Boston. They opened the bar and reopened the kitchen. There was this giant table full of people: all of his friends, his assistant, his publicist and the head of production for Warner Brothers. George ordered club sandwiches and French fries for everyone. He sat and told stories for hours. I was sitting next to his mom. It was crazy. It was an awesome, awesome time. That was a time when I was sitting there thinking, 'Gosh, what am I doing here?'

"Those experiences are great, but the novelty wears off after a while. You realize they are real people, they're just people."

M.C.'s job in publicity gives her the best of both worlds. "You get to have a fairly normal work schedule, you get holidays, 401(k) and a regular paycheck. You can have a normal existence, but you also have the glamour and excitement of the entertainment industry.

"I truly love film. I like working for a studio and I like the fact that the product I am promoting is a film. I love going to the movies and think it's a really important form of art. It wouldn't be as much fun for me if I was promoting pretzels or something."

M.C. has enjoyed working on some of the new-at-the-time films that have "pushed the envelope" for Warner Brothers, like *Syriana, North Country* and *V for Vendetta*. "I felt really proud to be part of the mechanism that brought important art out to the public."

I asked her what it took to excel in publicity and M.C. said there are three success factors. You need to be the kind of person who is organized, communicates well and builds relationships.

I asked M.C. to remember back to when she was trying to figure out what she wanted to do. She had done a lot of thinking and planning for her future. "First and foremost, listen to your gut. Observe yourself, what do you like to do on a day-to-day basis? I was someone who loved theater and film and movies. Sometimes you never think the things that are hobbies and are fun can actually be something you can do in life and make money."

She laughed, "I've been really lucky. Early on you really have to think about what you love doing and then research and investigate what opportunities there might be to work in and around that activity. You're going to work for the rest of your life and if it's something you're passionate about, it will be infinitely more fun and fulfilling."

She said different fields work for different people. "Everyone has a different trajectory. You have to prioritize what's most important for you in your day-to-day job and your day-to-day life. Is it your title? The money you're making? Your responsibility within your particular job? Is it the environment you're working in? I think you figure all of it out through trial and error."

In New York there is a lot of job hopping. M.C. did that at first, but then settled in when she found what she enjoyed at Warner Brothers. "I decided I worked in an environment I really liked, with people I really liked. It's motivating and inspiring to work with creative people. I like dealing with the press and coordinating details with them that ultimately end up becoming a really interesting appearance on TV or an interview in a magazine. I just happen to be at a place where I've built a lot of strong relationships over the years and feel comfortable."

The entertainment field is like a lot of others; chances are slim you'll walk into a job that pays a lot of money. "You definitely have to start at the bottom. I started out working for free as an intern at Letterman and for pennies as a CBS page. If it's something you want to do, then paying your dues is worth it. If you're excited about it and you're motivated and energized, that's the real payoff. We're all going to work for a long, long time, so you've got to keep it exciting."

• • • • • • • • • • • • • • • • • • • •

REWIND

- M.C. knew from the start that she wanted to work in the entertainment industry, she just didn't know how. Yet, because she knew what she wanted, M.C. was able to think long range. She worked for free. She worked for pennies. Those jobs gave her the experience and contacts to get into Warner Brothers. "If it's something you want to do, then paying your dues is worth it." Short term pain for long term gain.

- M.C.'s story also shows there are numerous ways to live your passion. "Sometimes you never think the things that are hobbies and are fun can actually be something you can do in life and make money." If you love movies (or anything), you may not get to be the "star," but there are a lot of other roles that still let you take part in your passion.

- Another lesson we can learn from M.C. is the importance of going on career "dates." Her experiences during her internships gave her the confidence to know what she wanted. "You just learn so much by being out there and doing and seeing." Look back on Lesson Four. What can you do to go on career dates?

- Lastly, M.C. says, "I like the fact that the product I am promoting is a film... It wouldn't be as much fun for me if I was promoting pretzels or something." She enjoys promotion, but gets more joy because she is working in her chosen field. Some people work in a role that uses their talents well, but can lose motivation if they aren't in a field they are passionate about or aren't working on a mission they believe in. Others feel "management is management," or "if I can sell Girl Scout cookies, I can sell time shares," and just delight in being good at what they do. It's important to see which way your motivations work.

CHAPTER TWENTY-SEVEN

Splits in the Road
Founding the 401(k) program

Most of us will come to a crossroads a few times in our lives. The decisions we make will have a profound impact on our future. Sometimes, as we ponder our choices, new opportunities present themselves. And our road becomes wider. This was the case for Ted Benna.

Leading up to a talk I was giving at Penn State, an attendee emailed me and told me I had to interview, "The father of the 401(k)," Ted Benna. She said he had a story about finances and faith that I would find interesting.

I had never heard of Ted before so I hopped online. In fact, this man who lived in a small town outside of Williamsport, Pennsylvania, was featured in *Money* magazine, *Fortune* and *USA Today* as the first to implement a 401(k) program.

I pulled up to his unassuming brick ranch home nestled next to a tributary of the Susquehanna River. Ted was a lanky six-one and his gray hair was free to do what it pleased. He wore washed out jeans and a faded green sweater that at one point may have had "Montana" printed on it. We walked around the modest house, which I ball-parked at around 2,500 square feet, and went into his study. Two of his four books, *401(k) for Dummies* and *Escaping the Coming Retirement Crisis* were in sight.

I started off with anxious pings of questions about the 401(k). Ted smiled a smile that said to be patient. "Andrew, the 401(k) is the most important event in my business life, but there is something even more important than that I want to share with you." And we started down his path of finances and faith.

Ted started his career in Philadelphia at Provident Mutual Life Insurance Company. Then he and three others started an employee benefits consulting firm, The Johnson Companies, which grew into a 350 person operation. "Up to that point I had become very good at helping people pay less tax, particularly doctors, professionals and small business owners. The problem was that most of them wanted me to design a plan where they got the biggest personal gain from it and gave the least to their employees. It was the nature of the beast and I knew how to do it well."

In his late 30s, Ted was at an intersection. "At age 37 or 38 I said, 'I don't think I want to come to the end of the road and say that's what I spent my life doing.' I was thinking of leaving the financial world for some type of ministry."

He then reflected back on his spiritual journey. In his mid 20s, Ted's faith was put to the test. He had grown up in a church, but as he attended with his wife and four young children, it was not connecting. "I came to the conclusion it wasn't doing anything; it wasn't making any difference in me or the lives of the other people that were attending. I said, 'Hey, I could be on the golf course or walking in the woods and have as much impact.'"

This disconnected feeling stayed with him until he heard two speakers at his church—both businessmen. The first shared his journey as a successful entrepreneur who had previously been on skid row. He had been an alcoholic and lost his family, business and home. At the time of the talk, the speaker had turned his life around and was sharing his testimony about his relationship with Jesus Christ. "It was evident that he had something going I didn't have. No doubt about it."

A few months later, the second speaker shared his spiritual journey. Ted heard the message differently than before. "For the first time, I actually recognized the truth. I had heard it before, but it was amazing to actually have the blinders removed to see what God sees in me. It was very painful at first because I came to the realization I was no better than the guy who had been in the gutter. But then they said, 'All have sinned and fallen short of God's glory.' Well, I was smart enough to realize all didn't allow for exception and that had to include me. It hit home. It finally clicked.

"I saw very clearly that I had a decision to make. The decision was to accept Christ as my lord and savior, or to turn my back and walk away. I understood the road, the split road; you could go either way, understanding the ramifications of the decision. Fortunately, I decided to accept Jesus at that point. It wasn't a 180 degree change. It was a journey that began and continues."

Ted's faith became the central part of his life. His financial business grew. But as he said previously, in his late 30s he was at a crossroads between finance and ministry. He tried to blend them together by exploring a business position within the Philadelphia College of the Bible (now Philadelphia Biblical University). He also did a lot of analysis and praying about what he should do. It was during a time of deep reflection in 1980 that the 401(k) plan came to him. His face beamed as he told me about it. "The myth is I was sitting reading the IRS code and discovered this paragraph no one had ever found before. That clearly isn't what happened. What happened was I interpreted that section in a very different way than what was intended."

Ted told *TIME* magazine his interpretation of the code. "Large employers at the time had retirement savings plans in which employees put in money after taxes and received a matching employer contribution. I realized it would be possible to change those plans so that employees would be able to put their money in before taxes rather than after."

And by interpreting the IRS code in a new way, the answer for what he should do presented itself. "That started my work in a very different direction. I was feeling better because I was helping people who really needed it. That was more fulfilling."

The father of the 401(k) explained the program. "401(k) is a plan for the average worker. It's really a plan for Middle America—for people making $20,000 to $100,000 a year. For them, it's a great program. For senior execs, it's no big deal. For people below $20,000, it doesn't work. It has been extremely beneficial to mid-America. We are what make America unique. All countries have the well-to-do and the poor. The difference with our country is its large middle-income population."

Ted's work morphed as he began to share the 401(k) plan with people and help them plan for retirement. In the beginning, he was met with skepticism. "Companies took care of their employees for life via their pensions. No one had heard of 401(k) or saving for retirement. Both of those were very foreign concepts."

The first article written about the 401(k) was in the *Philadelphia Inquirer* and it got picked up nationally. "They ran it on a Friday and by Monday they had hundreds of telephone calls saying it's not legal, you can't do it, etc. That was the first reaction."

During this time Prentice Hall published an executive newsletter series that went to CEOs, CFOs and other high level executives. Ted contacted them about the 401(k) and after sending in some information, they asked him to meet with them and explain the program in more detail. Rather than meeting with one writer, he was set up for a presentation in an auditorium. "These were the people who wrote about the tax law. I'm 39 years old and I get up in front of this who's who group. They had a negative attitude about them. It was funny though; about an hour into it, the discussion became focused on, 'How can we do this at Prentice Hall?'" he laughed.

Ted did not take credit for the 401(k), he gave the glory to God. "I knew the 401(k) was going to help a lot of people. I was pumped up because of it. What ultimately became clear was God saying, 'You don't have to go someplace else; I've given you a ministry where you are. You just need to be faithful where I have you.'"

Word of mouth on the 401(k) began to spread and Ted was recognized nationally. His call to ministry got him involved with the Christian Business Men's Committee. He would speak around the country, blending the most important event in his business life, the 401(k), with his most important faith life.

The media coverage boomed. Ted was featured as one of the eight most influential people in the financial world for *Money* magazine's 20th anniversary edition. He spoke openly about his faith in the media interviews. He smiled as he told me about the *Money* article. "Their headline was, 'His answer to prayer.' They worked my faith into the article. *Fortune* and *USA Today* did the same thing. It was amazing to see that happen."

From Ted's interpretation of the same paragraph that thousands of other financial analysts had looked at before, he's been able to help over 50 million people. He fidgeted so I guessed he was uncomfortable talking about himself for such a long period. "I've been able to do what I wanted, but do it in a different way than I thought."

We talked about the 401(k) for a few more minutes and then I shifted our conversation to my Work Equation. I spelled out the pieces of the equation and told him 84,000 hours of our life will be spent at work. Ted thought about it and smiled. "Andrew, that's pretty good, but I think your math is off a little bit. I don't think your generation will be retiring at age 65.

"What's happening now is the final phase of the demise of the pension systems. Retirement is a pretty new phenomenon in the history of mankind.

"Our Social Security system was started when the normal retirement age was 65. It was primarily a male workforce, largely industrialized and you had retirees typically living for 10 or 12 years. Now we've moved to 20-year, 30-year and longer retirement periods which are unsustainable. Society frankly can't afford to have a huge section of the population spending 30 years idle. It's untenable. But, we've unfortunately created that expectation, and what has happened at the corporate and government levels is the cost of a lifetime is grossly underestimated. The harsh reality is companies can't afford it."

He then predicted an upcoming generational tension between the older and the younger segments of the population in the 2020s. "You need to ratchet down expectations. There is this huge boomer population and it's no secret they are marching off to retirement. This is going to put unprecedented strain on government systems. Medicare is a huge problem. It's now in a negative cash flow. Social Security is projected to go negative around 2014 or 2015. The idea of people retiring at mid to late 50s or 60s and going off and spending 30 or 40 years in financially secure situations is probably going away. The boomers might be the last generation that is able to do that."

Ted reiterated that my Work Equation may be off. "The biggest thing is people are going to have to work longer."

If you like your work, that might be a positive. If you don't . . .

REWIND

- Ted was at a career crossroads. He came very close to leaving the financial world for ministry. During this time of analysis, he was blessed to have his established road widened through discovering and sharing the 401(k) option. "I've been able to do what I wanted, but do it in a different way than I thought."

  When thinking about your career, before you take a new turn altogether, take some time to reflect and ask how you might use your impetus for change and use that to widen your existing road.

- It is important to understand that the founder of the 401(k) told me my work equation is off and that we may have to work 94,000 hours or 104,000 hours in our life. This looks more and more realistic. Yet, the end solution to the work equation does not change. If you have to work 84,000 or 104,000 hours, if you are passionate about what you do, your time at work won't feel like a drag.

Note: The economic downturn of 2008, 2009 and 2010 produced a lot of talk about savings, retirement and the 401(k). I am not an economist, but I know that the 401(k) has helped millions of people for many years and will continue to be a resource in the future. Shady bankers and real estate executives may have impacted the stock market and caused some people to question their 401(k) plan, but if I can invest the money I make before it is taxed, I am glad someone figured out a way to do it.

LESSON TEN

How Bad Do You Want It?

Once you know what you want to do, you will likely have to navigate a bumpy road, full of ups and downs, before arriving at the point where you are fully living your purpose and passion. The ups are when you catch glimpses of your purpose and how you can live it. The downs are when you wonder if the sacrifices you are making are worth it. In the end, your passion and sense of purpose need to carry you through the pain.

You may have to pay your dues and work your way up like Mary Cameron VanGraafeiland, the movie publicist. You may have to take a job making much less than you are currently making, as Geoff Calkins did in becoming a sports columnist. Or you may have to take out loans to reach your dreams, as dressmaker Brooke Priddy did.

I have lived this lesson well. Once I left my sales job to go on the road, I saw my savings slowly drain down like the sand in an hourglass. My bank accounts were almost completely depleted, and it was time to ask myself, "Okay, now what am I supposed to do?" My dream job was to share the stories of the people I interviewed via this book and speaking engagements. But that's not something where you just snap your fingers and it happens. It couldn't pay the bills right away.

The state of my finances made me reflect. In Charlotte, I lived in a killer apartment in the heart of uptown. Returning from the road, I had to move back in with my parents. Then I rented a shoebox, studio apartment. In Charlotte, I used to be able to do just about anything I wanted without considering cost. On the road and while writing, I was forced to pinch every penny when it came to food, clothing and entertainment. In Charlotte, I had the freedom to travel wherever I wanted. My road trip took me to some great places, but when it was time to write this book, there were instances I could barely afford to fill up my gas tank.

In the down times, I asked myself two questions. The first was a version of, "What the hell are you doing?" Immediately or eventually, the second question would muscle its way into my consciousness. "Andrew, this is your dream. How bad do you want it?"

My circumstances had definitely changed, but the answer to question number two never did, "I want it bad. I have to make my dream a reality." No question it sucked being broke and it sucked not having the freedoms I used to have, but I knew that if I took the sales jobs I was being offered or took a job for the money as opposed to the passion, all of the travels, interviews and advice would lose their impact.

You will probably face similar crossroads on your journey. Should you proceed toward your passion or give in to the money? Should you press on even when times are tough, or cave to the pressure and do what others think you should do?

The answers will be different for each of us. I can say that I pressed on and I am grateful that I did. My passion propelled me through my pain. The following three chapters show how other people persevered to live their passion.

CHAPTER TWENTY-EIGHT

Doing Something Else to Get to Where You Want

In wine and in life, patience pays off

Many people I meet on the career road have a vision they want to achieve, but tell me they can't see the light at the end of the tunnel. They struggle with not being able to get to where they want to go "fast enough." In Penn Yan, New York, I sat down with Len and Judy Wiltberger, who chipped away for over 30 years to eventually make their vision of owning and running a vineyard into a reality.

On the way to the Wiltberger's I made my way through the Finger Lakes wine country of upstate New York. Van Morrison shouted over the wind barreling through my SUV's open windows and sunroof. I eventually saw the turnoff to Keuka Springs Winery and accelerated up a steep incline to the Wiltberger's wine making barn and tasting room.

I stared down the hill I had just climbed. Keuka Lake was like a blue bowl and the sun sparkled off the water. Small houses, bushy trees and green hills rose from the shoreline. I could see, but not hear, boats speeding by, pulling skiers. The splash of people jumping off a dock caught my eye.

I followed the signs past the back of the barn to the tasting room. Judy was mingling with some of the patrons, discussing one of the wines. She was five-two, tops, and had a big smile as she interacted with the customers. "Oh yes, this would go great with seafood," I heard her say to a woman sipping a glass of their white.

It was a warm day, so when asked by the person in the tasting room, I chose a white, Vignoles. I am not a connoisseur, but what I tasted was smooth and refreshing.

I then went outside to sit at one of the picnic tables and take in the view. Len, who is the same height as Judy, came outside shortly after. He said warmly, "Welcome. Let me show you around."

We surveyed the property from our picnic table vantage point. Looking out at the rows and rows of grapes, he said they were growing two types of red and four whites in the vineyard. The ideal weather for their grapes was warm days, cool nights and not a lot of rain. The Finger Lakes offered that. (Each wine region is different. Napa has warm days and warm nights.) "Cold climate growing regions tend to bring out the flavors in the fruit very dramatically," Len told me.

We went back into the tasting room and he poured me a glass of Clara's Red. He told me excitedly that they had opened the new barn, tasting room and wine press the previous year. We walked past Judy, the customers and the many bottles of wine into the back. Len explained, "Our business is still growing. We handle most of the operations by ourselves, including the bottling."

Before me was a bottling line machine about the size of a refrigerator on its back. He showed me large silver vats used to store the various wines. We weren't there long before he said, "Let's go outside."

I struggled to keep up as he walked quickly past the picnic benches and across the gravel driveway, hopped over a small brook and came to a stop amidst the grapes. The green vines were thin, flexible and leafier than I had expected. Next to their roots were wooden stakes and I could see the vines were all tied to a makeshift fence of parallel wires running between vertical poles, like a piece of sheet music with its staff and dividing measures.

"We use a technique called vertical shoot positioning," he said as he caressed one of the grapes. "It all starts in the winter, when the vines are dormant." With his hands Len made a cutting back motion as he described the need to trim, shape and prepare the vines for the growing season.

The key is sunlight. The way they set the plant up determines the exposure to the sunlight. "If you get great exposure, you get great wine. The more sun, the better."

He explained the trellis system that ran down each row. The vines were planted every eight feet and each was wired to grow upward into an area of three to six horizontal wires so that it would grow splayed out along a plane which faced the sun. "Each branch gets tied onto those wires. You have to hand do that to each one, like a twisty. It will hold the plant in the right way for maximum exposure."

I looked at the plant and imagined how much time and effort it must have taken to tie off the many branches for all the vines. He must have seen the expression on my face. "It's a ton of work. Anybody can grow grapes, but not everyone can have a great product in the fall for harvest."

It was close to 5:00 p.m. when the Wiltbergers prepared to close the tasting room. Once that was done, we drove down the hill, took a side road and arrived at their cottage. The rest of our talk took place at the shore of Keuka Lake, the view I had appreciated from the picnic table. The sun glistened off the water. Len and Judy came down carrying a bottle of white wine and three glasses. The water gently lapped on the pebbled shore. A slight breeze stirred the leaves of the tree they sat under. "It doesn't get much better than this," Len said as we toasted.

I asked them how the vineyard came to be and they laughed. "It wasn't easy," they said in unison.

Prior to the vineyard, Len had worked at Kodak and Judy was a teacher. They had four kids. Len explained that a number of factors had aligned to influence their decision. They had owned their cottage at the lake since 1969 and had a long-lived fascination with wine and wine making. In 1976 the New York State Legislature passed a Farm Winery Act that made it easier for farms and grape growers to open a winery. The year the law was passed, six wineries opened in the area and a seed was planted in their minds.

One of their neighbors was getting up in age and owned all of the land behind their cottage. She told them that 30 of her acres would be available and that if the land was used for agriculture, she'd sell it at a good price. They bought the land, which is now the hill with the grapes and tasting room. Judy added, "The original plan was to just grow grapes and sell them off for the kids' college fund."

After their first harvest, one of the vintners told them they had good grapes and that they'd be able to make saleable wine from them. Judy said, "The business side of things started in the early 80s when we planted the vineyard. Then in 1988 we opened a small tasting room in one of our neighbor's storage barns."

They loved life on the vineyard, but because of life responsibilities, Len and Judy couldn't put their entire focus on their wine. She explained, "If you have a family and kids, you have to balance it all out. Within your restraints, you make the best choices. We didn't go full force, full time because we had four kids to put through college and we didn't want to take the risk that wouldn't happen. There is nothing like a secure income. We thought we had a responsibility to them. We did what we could when we could."

Judy laughed. "Len was working full time at Kodak, I was teaching part time, and this occupied a lot of our time. In the years it was not profitable, there was a lot of stress. We didn't know how much longer we were going to keep going with it."

The Finger Lakes wine region was young when they started and there wasn't a lot of traffic. It was slow going. But after a few years, the region gained exposure and grew in reputation as a place to come for quality wine. Their business grew, allowing them to build the new tasting room. Len said, "It's like anything. There's an exponential curve that these processes go through. They start off slow and the slope picks up until it's kind of a critical mass, and once it gets past that, then it starts to go very steeply."

Judy added, "We were here when it was flat and we're thankful to see it turn. It's a really fun business to be in."

Len retired from Kodak two years prior to our talk, after 36 years of service. His newfound time has allowed them to develop their business. Prior to retiring, the focus was on the tasting room. Now they are selling more to stores. "I liked working at Kodak. I never had a bad year there. Without Kodak we never would've had the money to start this and the financial ability to do this. But, if you've ever worked for anybody for a long time, owning your own business is great."

They handle every aspect of the business and outlined for me three main phases: growing, processing and marketing. Keuka Springs has eleven employees. Two employees work in the vineyard and Judy manages the tasting room, which has nine employees. She enjoys her role. "Right now I like running the show, making the decisions and doing things the way we want them done. It's challenging because you're dealing with staff, you're dealing with the public, and there are all sorts of decisions for marketing and where you are going to spend your time and money; but they are our decisions."

The customers and the bottom line show them that they are doing well. Len shared their joy. "They come up to our place, look at the view and say 'Oh, my God.' When someone tries your wine at the tasting bar and you see them through the entire process, and they're just delighted with it, and they buy a case, there is immediate feedback." He looked at Judy, "It's very satisfying."

When asked, they wouldn't tell me which wine was their favorite. "That's like asking us to name our favorite child." The year of our interview, two of their wines had received double gold awards at a San Francisco judging. One of the two made it into the sweepstakes, which narrowed down 3,800 wines to the best 38.

As the sun set, they pronounced themselves very pleased with how they persevered. Len added, "From the vine to the bottle, we take the product all the way from its birth to where it's consumed. There are not many businesses where you can get the full life cycle and see the fruit being appreciated by somebody. It's very gratifying."

REWIND

- Len and Judy's passion for opening a winery was with them for over 30 years, but they attained it in stages. They worked at jobs other than the vineyard and put four kids through college, but they still kept the dream alive. "We did what we could when we could."

  On the road, if you have a vision but cannot do it full time, you still need to carve out a way to live it, even if it is for small amounts of time. Without getting a dose of your passion, you won't be fully happy. Any amount of time living your passion is better than no time at all.

  And who knows, if you plan, save, learn and grow, you might end up like the Wiltbergers. It took them 30 years, but their vision eventually evolved into something very special.

- As discussed in Lesson Seven, Len and Judy had a built-in support system—each other. Their relationship as a team allowed for different sacrifices to be made by each spouse as they worked toward their shared goal. Family life and putting their kids through college tempered their pace on the winery. By staying with outside employment, they avoided risking their children's educations, but still did what they could to keep their vision of owning a winery moving forward. Team is important. How would this have worked out if Len or Judy had the vision and the other one didn't?

CHAPTER TWENTY-NINE

Passion + Fear = Commitment

Spending six years and $500,000 to make a vision a reality

The struggle to achieve a dream takes many shapes and forms. In the case of Roger Bachman, his vision sailed into his life during a time of career turbulence.

Roger is the owner of Summer Wind Yacht Charters which operates out of Fort Lauderdale, Florida, in the winter and Rochester, New York, in the summer. Our interview took place in Rochester aboard his 53-foot catamaran, Wild Hearts. Leading up to our talk, the Rochester Fox News station contacted me to do an interview about my travels. I told them that my story is really about the people I interview, so I wanted to incorporate Roger and Wild Hearts into the piece. They agreed.

I met Roger for coffee prior to the news crew's arrival. He greeted me in a pair of shorts, top-of-the line sandals, long-sleeved t-shirt, hat and glasses. His mustache was finely trimmed.

Roger started by talking about his youth. "My passion for the water started at three years old. I sent a letter to the Navy at eight asking them how I could join. All I ever wanted to do was go to sea."

And he did. Although Roger had been accepted to numerous colleges and had a draft number of 324, which meant he probably would not be drafted, he enlisted in the Navy right out of high school and shipped out to Vietnam.

After Vietnam, Roger and a Navy buddy moved to Rochester. Roger attended the Rochester Institute of Technology for business, where he met his wife, Rosemary. After graduation, the newlyweds moved to Dallas, Texas, so Roger could work on his MBA.

Two of his younger brothers lived there and they asked Roger if he wanted to help them get a delivery company off the ground. "Ten years later we had the largest air freight company in Dallas with around 115 employees and all kinds of equipment. We were doing really, really well."

Then it was decision time. There were now four brothers working 18-hour days and they had to choose whether to expand the company or remain the same size. Because they chose to stay the same size, Roger thought they didn't need him anymore. Rosemary was homesick for Rochester, so they moved back and started over. "If you want to be happy in life,

you just have to go do those things. Everything that you have, whether it be nice furniture, nice things, it's all just stuff. For me, the ultimate risk is if you're willing to give up those comforts to do those things that you need to do or want to do."

Rosemary went to work in the insurance field and Roger excelled at sales and management jobs that had a common theme—develop a territory where a company had little or no market presence. Roger would start working for the company out of his house, and then grow the business to a small office, then a larger one and then oversee offices across the state. "I did it on a consistent basis and got a reputation as a guy who could grow a business."

Next, Thompson Publishing, a textbook company, hired him to kick-start their New York sales team. It was number 28 out of 28 locations. "Within two years we were able to get the New York sales team to the number two location," he said proudly.

Roger's niche as a start-up operations person for larger companies brought him plenty of money, but he didn't like the rules and restrictions that came with the success. "When you are a one-man operation, you can grow it and do what you want. People don't care as long as it's growing. When the operations start making a lot of money, then the restrictions start coming in. 'This is our new sales guideline policy and this is how it's going to be.' You have to conform. They start placing rules and restrictions on your ability to operate and maneuver. In fairness, a lot of those rules are probably good things, but I am not a person who likes that. I don't like to be hemmed in."

In 1998, Thompson Publishing wanted Roger to move to Seattle or Denver. Rosemary had a great job in Rochester and their two boys did not want to move. He wasn't sure what was next, but Roger told the company thanks but no thanks and took a severance package.

The next day Rosemary called him, told him to throw on some shorts and to meet her at the Port of Rochester to clear his head. "The schooner America had just pulled in that day. It's a replica of the very first boat that won the America's Cup [boat race] in 1851. I struck up a conversation with the captain and crew. The next day I left and went sailing as part of the America's crew for a month and a half on their Great Lakes tour."

Roger's family lived off his severance and Rosemary's income as he crewed on the America off and on for six months. It was during this time that Roger saw an opportunity. "The lines were two blocks long just to board her, never mind to sail on her. There was a huge demand for this as a product in the Great Lakes area. I thought, 'Well, there's got to be an opportunity here somewhere.' That's how I knew what I wanted to do, which was buy the America and take people sailing."

The vision took shape, but due to health and financial reasons, the vision did not blossom overnight.

Roger went back to developing new business territories, this time for Roto-Rooter. His attention was not focused on the boat for two years. But once he grew the Roto-Rooter business, the rules and regulations followed and he once again became frustrated. "In year three I altered the plan slightly and really began to look at building a schooner like the America."

He created a business plan, got boat specs from MIT, picked out a boat and went through the estimates of getting it built, all while trying to figure out a way to make it happen financially. "I went six ways to Sunday, and we couldn't make a tall ship work. In order to sail a boat like this you need a captain and at least eight crew. That's high on labor cost and the amount of upkeep on it, never mind that the cost of fuel and everything else, was very high. If you have a bad year and you need parts or have personnel issues, you're going to take it right on the chin and it's going to be a tough go."

Many of the people he talked to told him he needed to check out catamarans. "I am a monohull sailor. To me catamarans were a sellout."

He fought the catamaran plan and tried to make the numbers work. But after two years of planning, he relented. "From a dream standpoint it was nice, but it was not going to pay the rent. The initial vision was the America, but the numbers didn't add up. You have to be realistic about your dream. I asked, 'What else can I do to help me get there?'"

The numbers worked for a catamaran, so he conceded. Roger, his sister and a business partner flew to St. Croix, Maryland and Puerto Rico to look at new boats. In St. Croix, Roger got affirmation on his vision from the owner of a major boat manufacturer. Roger explained, "He told us, 'That's got to be the best business plan of any I've heard.'"

They bought Wild Hearts in Puerto Rico, but there were still doubts. "We pulled out of the Virgin Islands and sailed past the Dominican Republic in the new ship. I woke up in the middle of the night and said, 'Oh my God, I just spent over half a million dollars, I'm sailing this boat to New York... what if I'm the only one who thinks this is a good idea?' That was the unknown. I knew it was the right idea, but could I convince everybody else it was the right idea?"

It was six years of ups and downs from Roger sailing the America in 1998 to having his own ship and opening the charter business in July 2004 at the Port of Rochester.

We talked about his perseverance for his vision. "You can't let fear get in the way. This was an obvious risk, which was scary, but my health issues showed me that you can't wait forever or for the perfect moment. My health pushed me beyond the fear that comes with taking a big risk. And the fear of failure pushed me to make sure that I did all that I could to make this a success.

"You have to know in your heart it's the right thing to do. You have to be passionate and you have to be willing to risk everything in order to do it. There are times I come back and think to myself, 'You've just spent over $500,000, you have two boys who still have to go to college, you have a nice house, you have all of these things, are you 100 percent sure that this is the right thing to do?' Absolutely! No question about it. If you can answer that and you're willing to commit yourself to that kind of a risk, then by all means go for it."

Sailing gives Roger a unique perspective. "The water gives me clear thoughts and clear presence of mind. Every time I come back in, I am more motivated knowing I am on the right track, and I can't get sidetracked or take no for an answer."

And now Roger gets to share his passion for the water with others. "So many people are stuck in the same rut doing the same thing. The boat will get your blood stirring and your emotions going."

It sounded like there were quite a few naysayers during his journey to start the business. One of the most rewarding moments was when his mother came up from Dallas. She sat on the boat, got on her cell phone, called her sisters and told them that they were wrong; she was about to go out on Roger's boat. He laughed. "Just because it's different doesn't mean you can't go and do it."

Roger overcame a lot of adversity to see his vision come to life. He could have had a great living as the sales guru that took underdeveloped territories and grew them, but that did not bring him the fire. "You've got to be passionate about what you're doing. If you don't enjoy doing what you're doing, figure out what it is you want and go for it. What will happen is that you will catch glimpses. I catch glimpses of brilliance when I see the boat pulling in to dock and there are people gathered just watching us coming in and going out. That's when I know I am on the right track. You've got to do the research and then be willing to take that big of a risk."

As we wrapped up our conversation, the vision of the America from 1998 still tugged at Roger. He took out a picture of the vessel and explained that they were looking to expand to four catamarans in the Great Lakes. "There is no way a tall ship can make money by itself, but four catamarans could support a tall ship. I'll have my tall ship. That's still the goal," he said with a glow.

The Fox News crew arrived not too long afterwards and filmed us doing our interview. Later that night, our story was broadcast on the news. They started with Roger, Rosemary and I on the bow of Wild Hearts.

Then they cut to a clip of Roger. He said, "You need a healthy dose of passion, but more importantly you need fear. Fear is going to allow you to make the commitment to your dreams." Then they cut to Rosemary, "Pursue your dreams. Don't wait until tomorrow to do it, you don't know what tomorrow will bring."

• • • • • • • • • • • • • • • • • •

REWIND

- Many of us have a version of Roger's tall ship in our minds. It's probably not a boat, but it is a vision of where we want to go. But just because we have a vision doesn't mean we can flip a switch and it instantly materializes. Roger wanted to buy the America and take people sailing on it, but the numbers didn't work. "From a dream standpoint it was nice, but it was not going to pay the rent. You have to be realistic about your dream. I asked, 'What else can I do to help me get there?'"

  Roger's six-year journey combined his passion with research and planning. He was able to move forward in the shorter term because his business plan gave him the confidence to risk $500,000 on Wild Hearts. His boat brings in money every day taking people sailing. In the long term, he still has his sights set on a tall ship.

- If you have the passion but no plan, you can still take a risk. But your chances of success diminish greatly. Do your best to take educated risks. If the research shows your plan has a high probability of failure, and experts in the field see the same thing, be careful. At the same time, if you have a lingering fear that not living your passion will be your downfall, it is better to have tried and failed than to have never tried at all... but, you might try to keep the risk under half a million dollars if you can...

CHAPTER THIRTY

A Late Start is Better Than No Start

Becoming the first ever

Typically, after I give a talk, people come up to me and tell me about their lives, their struggles and their dreams. I love the feedback and the stories. In many instances, the person (young, old, male or female) will say, "I wish I could be a (insert dream job here) but I can't because..."

That is when I go into more detail on the story of Betty Dickey, the first ever female Chief Justice of the State Supreme Court of Arkansas. She helps me tell people, "You can because..."

My day in court took place in Little Rock, Arkansas. The downtown transformation of my college city since my graduation in 1998 was evident as I drove past the pristine Clinton Library and the restaurants of the Riverwalk. The pillars of justice ushered me into the mammoth court building on Marshall Street.

Court was about to be in session. I sat down in an area marked off by a wooden railing next to the judge's assistant. As I sat down, the bailiff bellowed, "All rise." In walked a judge. And another. And another. Chief Justice Dickey was in the center and because of the distance, it was hard to gauge her height. In comparison with the other judges, the Chief Justice was short, maybe five-three, and very trim. Her graying hair contrasted against her black robe.

The session covered two cases and lasted two hours. After the conclusion of arguments and a lunch recess, I entered Chief Justice Dickey's chambers. She wore a black suit and was sitting at a wide desk that was loaded with numerous, overflowing files. The American flag was on her right and the Arkansas state flag on her left. From close up, it was evident her eyes were focused and sharp. She got up from her desk and shook my hand. We sat at a table to the left of her desk, close to a window that was covered by thick, soft grey-blue curtains.

It turned out that medicine, not law, was her passion early on. Yet, society and life responsibilities dictated what she did (and didn't do) with her interest.

Chief Justice Dickey talked about how women of her generation got married and were supposed to stay at home, doing wifely and motherly things. "I didn't have children for several years so I wanted to go on and continue my pre-med work," she said. Her tone changed ever so slightly. "But my husband was opposed to it. So I didn't. We adopted a child and then had the other three." She showed me a picture of them.

When the kids were out of elementary school, Chief Justice Dickey's husband told her she needed to go to work. She laughed, "I have four children and a foster child. I have been working."

The bookkeeper at her husband's law office had recently left, and because she knew the ins and outs of the firm, she filled that position. She also decided to go to law school. "I was over 40 when I started law school. The kids were very supportive of me working and I actually found it was easier than staying home."

Chief Justice Dickey's days were very busy as she commuted to law school and managed one of the family businesses, a local Baskin-Robbins ice cream store. She enjoyed law school. "I really liked the criminal law part of it and eventually opened my own office." Her husband still had his own firm, but they decided it would be better if they didn't practice together.

Her career continued to evolve. She started her public service as the assistant city attorney in Pine Bluff, Arkansas as well as the city attorney of Redfield, Arkansas. Later she joined a Little Rock firm and then became Little Rock's city attorney. From there, she blazed a new trail by running for state prosecutor. "I ran because the prosecutor before me was not doing his job. It was kind of a surprise that I won. I was the first woman elected prosecuting attorney in the state," she added with a smile.

In her third and fourth years as state prosecutor (1997 and 1998), she was part of two high profile cases. The first was against a lawyer who milked his clients out of $8 million to support a gambling habit. Because of the notoriety from the win, she was asked to be special prosecutor on a Boy Scout pedophile case. The case ran on the news all over the United States because they were able to identify 100 kids he had molested.

Chief Justice Dickey described the cases. "In the first case, the lawyer wanted to plead in federal court because he knew it was a white-collar crime and he'd get about five years. I persuaded the U.S. attorney to allow me to try him in the state court. He got 156 years. And then the Boy Scout pedophile got four life's plus 80 years for what he had done. It was a significant victory."

While trying the pedophile case, Governor Mike Huckabee asked if she would run for Attorney General. She did and lost, but was appointed to the Public Service Commission. Then, the Governor asked her to be his chief legal counsel. That was the first time a woman had been chosen for that slot. "That was a good first."

We paused for a moment. "And this job; in the history of the court, they'd never had a woman Chief Justice," she gleamed.

I asked how she made the change from an interest in the medical field to that of law. Her years of marriage to a lawyer piqued her interest in law, particularly the criminal side. "It's an area you can get your arms around as far as trying cases. It's not complicated like tax or some other areas."

Criminal law gave her a sense of purpose. "It appeals to the nurturing instinct of a woman because it's protecting the victims. Quite often we were doing as much work trying to stop a murder as we were trying to prosecute one, particularly when it was a domestic violence issue."

Since she became Chief Justice, she's had to change her way of looking at things. "Instead of being an advocate like a prosecutor is, as a judge, I'm balancing the interests or protecting the constitutional rights of the defendant. I've had to adjust my thinking. It is a fascinating job."

We returned to discussing her choice of law over medicine and she paused in thought. "I got a law degree because my husband said I had to go back to work. We're no longer married, but we're still friends. We have our children. It's really interesting to analyze, how did I get here?" We both laughed.

Then there was a silence. Her voice slowed. "Life is what happens to you while you're planning your life. Raising my children was the most challenging and gratifying career I've had. It took me so long to get here.

"It's important to do what you like to do. I wish that I had stronger knowledge of the law, but I've practiced almost 20 years. I've had to overcome some adversity. All of us go through difficulties. We cannot be made bitter by the bad things that happen."

Through participating in so many cases, she has met a lot of people in the law field and in politics. "There are so many people that I see doing what they think will make them the most money. They say they want to go into politics and they want to run for something. The pursuit of money or the pursuit of political power—I think it's wrong. It's doing what makes you happy and what gives you a sense of fulfillment."

She told me emphatically, "What you ought to do is make a change to society for the better. If you like what you do and are good at it, and then people look at you and think you're a worthy candidate for office, that's when to run. We are so blessed. It's important that you give something back."

It was obvious she was driven by wanting to make a change for the better. "I ran for prosecutor because I couldn't get anyone to run and the prosecutor before me had some personal problems. The office was not being run right. I saw a problem that needed to be fixed.

"If you don't see a problem that needs to be fixed, or a cause that's worth taking on or an adventure worth taking, you're going to look back and be very unhappy," she said, and then paused to take a breath.

Then the conversation segued into an unexpected topic: Tim McGraw. "There is a great song, 'Live Like You Were Dying.' You've got to live life to the fullest. That song is about going skydiving or mountain climbing or whatever. You ought to live like it's a gift for you to enjoy."

Her lips pursed and her eyes squinted in concentration. "Life is not a power struggle. It's not all about money, or how much stuff you collect. You need to recognize that things are not as important. This job, as great as it is—if I were not successful as a mother, I don't think I'd have it in me. I took on that responsibility. I accepted it. I had a duty to serve and give back."

We shifted gears and she talked about her faith and spirituality. "That part of your life is so important. So are what you do in response to your faith and how you live your life and what you do for other people."

She laughed. "Who knows where we lead next. Doors are open for you. If you don't have an adventuresome spirit or aren't brave enough to go through those doors, you will miss out. If you live your life in the shadows or in the shallow water, you'll never know what it's like down river."

Where we go next depends on us.

REWIND

- Betty Dickey's journey shows how a woman who was once strongly discouraged from working can knock down doors and become a trailblazer. In the history of Arkansas, she became the first female prosecuting attorney, first female chief legal counsel to the Governor and first female Chief Justice of the Supreme Court. She did not gain those titles by craving power or money. Her passion to fix problems came through in her actions, which led powerful sponsors to select her for the pioneering positions.

- Every goal you set for yourself will also uncover potential reasons to give up. The ability to see past those supposed obstacles is what separates Chief Justice Dickey from most. It is easy to say, "I can't because... (I'm a woman, I have children, I'm over 40, I have no experience or education in that field...)" It takes courage to say, "I will because..."

- As we progress down our own career roads, what started out as our dream may change. Life can introduce us to interests and options that had not occurred to us before. And sometimes, "finding a problem that needs to be fixed," can lead to a career, if you are suited for the work.

- Chief Justice Dickey also shows that it is never too late to start on the road to loving your career and life. Realize that the Chief Justice of the state Supreme Court of Arkansas started law school after age 40! It doesn't matter if you're age 20, 40, 60 or 80. The key is to let your passion out and simply—start.

LESSON ELEVEN

Make a Difference

When I tell people about my book and talks, they typically ask me for advice on careers. Sadly, there is no magic formula I can share with them. What I do tell them is that the single most common factor for job satisfaction throughout all of my research and interviews is that people who love their jobs feel like they are making a difference in some shape or form.

As Betty Dickey just told us, "If you don't see a problem that needs to be fixed, a cause that's worth taking on or an adventure worth taking, you're going to look back and be very unhappy."

The stereotype of making a difference is curing cancer or moving to an impoverished nation and volunteering your time. The reality of making a difference is that each of us has been blessed with unique talents and aspirations. You make a difference by using your natural gifts and abilities. You make a difference by having passion for your job and for your life. You make a difference by being happy at work and at home. You make a difference by being a living example for others.

And yes, you may cure cancer, save people from burning buildings or teach people to read. But you also may be a tree pathologist, maintenance person or music composer. It's not necessarily about the career you choose, it's about how you feel doing it.

I like the way Geoff Calkins says it. "If you love any job and you bring enthusiasm and energy to it, and it's your passion... it has an impact. You're going to bring something to it and you're going to make a contribution."

Mark my words, if you love what you do for a living, you will make a difference in the world. You may impact one person or you may impact one million people. The way I see it, if everyone was living their purpose and with passion, the positive Ripple Effect would be incredible and the world would be an amazing place.

The following four people show how making a difference in other people's lives makes a difference in their own.

CHAPTER THIRTY-ONE

The Rush to Help Others

Responding to the 9/11 attacks

When I was a child, one of the things I thought about becoming was a firefighter. In Alexandria, Virginia, I met with Joe Merritt, a firefighter and medic. He filled me in on what the day-to-day life of a firefighter is like and about his experience responding to the 9/11 attacks on the Pentagon. It turned out I was also able to live a childhood dream.

I pulled into the Fairfax County Fire and Rescue Station Number 11. My research said Fairfax County was one of the top fire and rescue units in all of the United States. Joe showed me around the station and introduced me to a few people. It seemed like everyone had a nickname. He was Big Joe and there was Red Dog and also Gump.

My plan had been to interview Joe and move on to the next city. But as we were deciding where to set up for the interview, a loud alarm went off. A siren beeped three times. Then a fuzzy, female voice came over the loudspeaker and rattled off names and numbers that had no meaning to me.

Her words did mean something to Joe. He looked at me and beckoned hurriedly, "Are you ready? Let's go!" I wasn't sure what he meant and didn't say anything. "C'mon, stay with me," he said. We ran out a door to a medic unit. He opened the side door and directed me to the back seat, which faced the gurney. I buckled up as Joe slammed the door. My heart pounded.

The big garage door swung up and the sirens blared. I had my back to Joe and Bill, the driver. Bill shifted the gargantuan vehicle into herky-jerky gear and we merged into traffic. I stared out the back window of the medic unit as we made our way through traffic. Joe told me to put on a headset similar to those worn by NASCAR pit crews. I could hear Joe and Bill talking. They told me not to hit the red button on the right side

Bill and Joe at the fire and rescue station

of the headset because it would transmit what I said back to base. The sirens wailed as I learned we were going to a call for an older male who had complained of dizziness.

After five minutes, we came to a halt. Joe and Bill hopped out. I unbuckled my seatbelt and waited, unsure of what to do next. Then, Joe opened my door and handed me an orange vest with "Fire and Rescue" printed on the back. "Follow me, but don't touch anything," he said. I hopped down and followed him up the sidewalk to the house with butterflies soaring in my stomach.

Joe changed into a different person as we approached the house. At the station he was laid back and mellow, but now he was in business mode. A young kid around 10 years old answered the door. Joe nicely, but systematically, grilled him with questions. "Who made the call? What is it for? Where is your grandfather?"

Some of the other firefighters were there along with the captain. To my surprise, the captain came over to me, and pointing to a spot near the front door, said, "Stay over there." He spoke in a friendly way, implying, "This will be a good vantage point." Joe and Bill went inside and I did as I was told.

An African-American man, who I assessed by his gray hair to be in his 70s was carried out on a stretcher by Joe and Bill. A couple of the others helped guide them down a few stairs and past me. I followed and stood behind the stretcher as they loaded the man into the parked medic unit.

Joe took my seat and assessed the patient by asking numerous questions and monitoring his heart. Joe had a very calming presence. He got up from the seat and said to the man, "Sam, this is Andrew. He's going to ride with you to the hospital."

As Joe passed me, I grabbed him, and with a look of fear, whispered, "What am I supposed to do?"

"Just sit there and talk to him," he said with a smile.

I secured my seat belt and sat facing Sam as the sirens roared en route to the hospital. I didn't show the awkwardness and panic that threatened to overcome me as I calmly asked Sam about his grandson and a few other things. He was responsive but it was obvious he didn't feel well.

We got to the hospital and Joe was in his element. When we wheeled Sam in, Joe knew a lot of the people in the ER. He gave a fist bump to one of the guys. He said hello to some of the doctors and nurses. Joe got Sam situated and completed a lot of paperwork (the one job task of which he was not a big fan). After 30 minutes we said our goodbyes to the staff and to Sam. "You're in good hands here," Joe said to Sam as he introduced him to the fist bump guy.

Joe and Bill disinfected and restored the back of the medic unit, and we returned to the station. It was dinner time when we arrived and I was surprised to learn that when possible, everyone at the station ate dinner together. There were 13 of us sitting around the table, talking and laughing as we ate. Gump, a rookie, had prepared broiled chicken, salad and a vegetable. The guys laughed and warned me the chicken was a bit, shall I say, "rare."

I sat at one end of the table, between Joe and Captain Walsh. Over dinner the captain quizzed me on my travels and interviews. He seemed to be genuinely intrigued and asked where I was going after dinner and my interview with Joe. I didn't have a plan or a place to stay. The Captain said, "Why don't you stick around and follow Joe for the shift? We can set you up a bunk here."

I was like a kid in a candy store. Nothing could wipe the smile off my face. I was now going to tail Joe and Bill for the entire shift, which ended at 7 a.m. They made up a bunk for me. I was now a firefighter for the night.

After cleaning up the kitchen, Joe and I found an empty office and sat down to do our interview. Seeing him on the job provided so much insight into his passion.

Joe was originally from Memphis, Tennessee. He said a very difficult experience at an early age showed him what he wanted to be. "Me and my little brother, Hank, used to go to Germantown (a suburb of Memphis) and ride on the fire trucks.

"Then Hank got hit by a car." By the tone of Joe's voice and the look on his face, I don't think Hank survived. I didn't ask. "The same rescue vehicle I used to work on in Germantown, Hank was one of their first calls. I had that in my mind. And I always liked helping people."

Joe went to college at Memphis State and got his BS in Emergency Medical Services (EMS). During school he got involved in the sheriff's rescue squad. "I liked it and started the career path."

He could not do enough to satisfy his appetite for learning. He was part of the first recruit school at the Germantown Fire Department, rode on the sheriff's squad and focused on EMS and extraction (the Jaws of Life). "I became a paramedic at the end of 1992 and loved being a firefighter/medic in Germantown. I got involved with everything. I went to every class I could get my hands on or they'd send me to. I enjoyed helping people and the thrill and rush of being a firefighter paramedic: the lights and sirens, pulling up, being in charge, being able to make a difference."

His superiors saw the passion Joe brought to his job and in 1993 the chief asked him to go to medical specialist classes in Rockville, Maryland, put on by the Urban Search and Rescue (USAR) team. USAR units rescue people in large buildings or structures that have collapsed due to earthquakes, hurricanes, tornadoes, bombs or other reasons.

FEMA had designated Memphis as one of 25 new domestic USAR teams to start around the country. "The classes were incredible."

Joe learned what happens to buildings once they get past a certain point and destruct. There were modules on how to navigate through debris, and how to rescue and treat the injured. "It was a whole week of the who's who of Search and Rescue and me, this 24-year-old kid. All the current top guys of USAR and the leading doctors were there. It was very interactive. We practiced in confined spaces and in damaged structures being cleared. It was a little overwhelming, but it was fun and it really got me excited about my work."

Joe and Dr. Joe Jolly helped set up USAR in Memphis. The contacts he made from the classes eventually led him to Fairfax. "They were one of the best USAR teams in the world. I had a big mouth and said I wanted to come to work for them. That's the kind of stuff I wanted to do, but still get to be a fireman in a big, progressive city."

Joe made his first USAR mission in 1999 when he went to Kenya after the seven-story embassy building had been blown up. He has been deployed to Taiwan for earthquake recovery as well as to hurricane sites. "It is pretty awesome to be able to help at that level."

At this point, the look on Joe's face changed. He stopped looking at me and around the room. His gaze was focused on the desk, like a child entranced by a television program. He was quieter. "There've been proud moments. There've been sad moments. 9/11 at the Pentagon was one of the biggest ones. We got called in three hours after it happened, when the side of the building collapsed. I wish I could show you the photo albums," he said solemnly.

"We went to my station where the USAR equipment was kept and loaded up on two buses, a tractor trailer, two support trucks and a police escort. Every street inbound to DC was closed. Every street outbound was bumper to bumper with people trying to get out," he recounted.

He was still focused on the desk. He did not smile. "When we came out of the station, looking over at the cars, and saw people scared and crying, it was tough. When the people saw us with the red and white USAR logo, their faces changed."

That change on the people's faces brought purpose to Joe. "When we got to the Pentagon, the guys who had been there first, fighting to save people, were whipped. A disaster the magnitude of the Pentagon was something most of them hadn't seen before. We had been to multiple, massive sites and this was devastating. We piled in there, found our spots, jumped off and went to work like madmen."

His voice rose in volume slightly. "You could tell it energized the people. You could see it in their eyes. It regenerated them. It was awesome."

His focus was still locked on the desk. "I remember seeing their faces and those of all the people driving down there," he said in almost a whisper. We didn't talk for a few seconds and then he lifted his gaze back to me.

Joe was injured at the Pentagon and during recovery, he went to a 9/11 press conference at the White House. He was one of four firefighters in the Roosevelt Room with New York Governor George Pataki, then-Governor of Pennsylvania Tom Ridge, Governor of Virginia Jim Gilmore and the head of the Red Cross. President George W. Bush came in and spoke to the group for a few minutes. After the press conference one of the President's aides directed the four firefighters into the Oval Office. "We walked in and there was President Bush at his desk. It was the four of us, Bush and a photographer. No Secret Service. They shut the door and he gave us all hugs. We talked with him for about 15 minutes, just like me and you," he said with pride.

We talked about why Joe comes to work. "Being a firefighter and a medic, I have the opportunity to get up every day and come and help people. You want to be here. You don't want to call in sick. You don't want to miss a day. It's so much fun. The activity makes it a job you really do enjoy. The thrill of it: the driving, the fire trucks, putting out fires, saving people from heart attacks. Every day you don't know what you'll get. Every minute it could be something totally off the wall. If there is no one else, who are you going to call? The fire department. We'll come, and we'll help you.

"A lot of people take a job just for a paycheck. For the true folks, you just want to be able to help. I'm doing my job here to help out, same thing as a soldier. To do some of the stuff we do, you have to be a little crazy. It's scary and you have to rely on your team. Male, female, black, white, Asian, Hispanic, I don't care who you are, as long as you can do the job. If I don't work hard, I feel bad because I'm letting other people down. It's a thrill. Going into burning buildings, riding on the fire boat, doing water rescues, rappelling off of buildings, helping with massive car wrecks, it's controlled chaos.

"Being a good firefighter is relying on your team. When we lose people, you typically don't see only one person, it's usually two or three. Why? Because we're in there together. Most of us are here because we want to help people and for the thrill of the job."

I equated being a firefighter and controlling chaos to like being on an athletic team. It just takes one weak link to cause dire consequences. The consequences are even greater on this team. If you screw up, the problem is not that the other team will score a goal, a basket or a touchdown; people may die. That fear brings stress, focus and camaraderie. It also brings the thrills that Joe talked about.

Joe looked out the window. "It's interesting. The things that I've done over 14 years; the people that I've seen and met, the lives I've touched, I could quit today and be happy that I've done a good job. I lay down a while back and thought about how many calls I'd run in 14 years: 8,000, maybe 10,000 people. How many fires? How many lives?" he reflected.

"In today's world, you've got to do the job you really want. It's funny being around DC and all of the political people. The things I do compared to what they do; their riches will never compare to what I have. I think someone who deals with life and death on a daily basis looks at things differently than most. So many people do something for a paycheck, or because they have to or because they don't think they can do anything else. Take the risk. Take the chance."

He looked directly at me. He spoke very seriously, "I enjoy it. I don't know how I could do another job."

Our interview was concluding when the alarm went off and the female voice called Joe's code again. For the rest of the shift, I was Joe's shadow. We went to three calls. My most intense moment was during a call for a woman who had suffered a stroke while at church. Joe said if you can catch a stroke in the first hour, you can minimize the damage. I was in the back of the medic unit with Joe as he was in action mode. Bill bobbed and weaved the ambulance towards the hospital. I held her hand and tried to calm her as we sped against the clock.

REWIND

- My shift with Joe is one of my favorite memories from the creation of this book. I learned that being a firefighter takes a lot of effort, training, dedication, perseverance and caring. Joe showed me that when you feel like you are making a difference, it is easier to learn more, work harder and do things most people won't.

- A theme that seems to run deep in a lot of the people I met that day is summed up by Joe's quote: "Being a firefighter and a medic, I have the opportunity to get up every day and come and help people."

Emergency personnel like the rush of the different calls, but it is helping people that brings them and keeps them in this profession. The passion Joe and the team possess is not built around money or power. Their purpose is helping people. And they live their purpose every day.

CHAPTER THIRTY-TWO

Changing People's Paradigm
The Nelson Mandela effect

Many of us put pressure on ourselves to change the world. We define that to ourselves as large-scale change, with a capital "C." The key is to figure out how we can do that in our own way. In the case of Dr. Paula Newsome, she blazed a trail as a woman and an African-American. Her story contains a lot of soul-searching to decide if she should change careers to help fix a country.

Dr. Newsome was my optometrist when I lived in Charlotte, North Carolina. In between our conversations of, "Better 1 or Better 2?" and, "What can you read on that line?" we would talk about work and life. She always made an impression on me—and I could tell she loved what she did. I could tell it in her answers to my questions and in the caring way she interacted with her patients. She took interest in me beyond my eyes. I also found out that she was involved in many volunteer activities. Once I decided I was going on the road to interview people, Dr. Newsome was tops on my list.

We met in the conference room of her two-story, 8,000 square feet practice. It was 10:15 a.m. and I could tell she was at full throttle. "Hi Andrew, sorry for the wait, it's been crazy," she said with an outstretched hand.

Dr. Newsome is slightly taller than I am, around five-eleven. She wore a white doctor's coat over a red turtleneck sweater. Her dark hair was pulled back high and her milk-chocolate skin glowed beside the white of her coat. We sat down and she talked about her career road.

Growing up in Wilmington, North Carolina, Dr. Newsome was an avid dancer and in toe shoes by age 12. She had visions of being a professional ballerina until a five-inch growth spurt brought on Osgood-Schlatter disease, a bone disease in the knee that occurs in young athletes. She had to stop dancing and wear a cast from her ankle up to her thigh. She said, "Maybe I'm not going to be a prima ballerina and I need to come up with a back-up career."

From that point on she was drawn to service fields. "I knew I wanted to help people."

The idea of being a doctor or scientist intrigued her. "My father was a hunter and I would always help him clean up the animals when he brought them home. I always liked science and trying to figure out stuff. I knew that blood, guts and all of that stuff did not bother me," she explained in her quiet, melodic voice.

She focused on science during high school and enrolled at the University of North Carolina at Chapel Hill in biology and pre-med. She received her optometry degree and went into practice. Yet, in 1984, optometry was still uncharted territory for a woman and even more so for an African-American.

We didn't go into a lot of depth on the racial prejudice she faced, but in an article I read in the *Review of Optometry*, one instance summed up her initial job search. Dr. Newsome had sent out a lot of resumes and by her name it was obvious she was a woman, yet not so obvious she was African-American. In one case, she went on an interview, shook the hand of the doctor, and was quickly told they had no suitable positions available for her. She wondered, "If there were no openings, why are they interviewing people?"

Experiences such as that mixed with an entrepreneurial drive helped motivate Dr. Newsome to open her own practice. "It was hard. First of all banks weren't used to having women ask them for money for practices. They didn't have a model or prototype. This was before it was against the law for them to ask about if you were planning on having a baby and those kinds of things—which they did ask me: 'Are you planning on having children? Are you planning on doing this full time? Is this just a hobby for you?'"

At that time, she was engaged and the banks thought her fiancé would run the practice. That was definitely not the case. She eventually received the funding and now runs a $2 million practice.

"I am actually the first African-American female to own her own optometry practice in the state of North Carolina." Dr. Newsome is also the first African-American woman to become a fellow in the American Academy of Optometry.

She didn't rehash her battles, just the joy she gets from working. "It's not a chore for me to get up in the morning and come into work. I love making people see better. I love taking care of eyeballs," she giggled. "As a testimony to that, I work for free at least once or twice a year doing mission work outside of the United States."

Her mission work began after meeting a legend. "In 1990, Nelson Mandela got out of jail and came to the United States. I had a friend who said they were able to get me in to meet him personally. They literally called me and told me to get on the next plane, and I was on the next plane to Los Angeles. I went to the L.A. Coliseum and was backstage with all these celebrities; 80,000 people were in the stands.

"His presence was so just awesome and awe-inspiring. He had such a sense of peace and sense of calm about him."

I thought Dr. Newsome had a similar sense of peace and calm about her.

The next day her hotel phone rang at 7:30 a.m. "My friend said, 'I can get you in to meet Mr. Mandela. You have to be ready in 30 minutes,'" she said and then laughed. "I was still in bed."

Luckily she was staying at the same hotel, the Biltmore. She got ready and went to his suite. Everyone there was looking for pictures or one-on-one time with him. "He didn't want that because he had just gotten up. He had just finished eating breakfast and wanted to chill out."

She talked in an even slower tempo than before. "I was just sitting there, enjoying being in the room with him. Everyone else was trying to take pictures. I was there to be in his presence. I just wanted to see the man up close."

Her face was radiant. "He looked at me and said, 'And so, what is your name?' I told him. 'What do you do?' And I told him. He said, 'We need eye doctors in my country.' I said, 'I'm sure you do, Mr. Mandela.' And he said, 'Well, would you like to take a picture with me?' And I said, 'Mr. Mandela I would be honored to take a picture with you.'" She let out a big happy laugh. "He was calling me Dr. Newsome. I said, 'You don't have to do that, call me Paula.'"

Dr. Newsome was the only person in the entire three-room suite to get a picture with just the two of them. Three or four months after their meeting one of her medical journals came in the mail; it stated they needed optometrists to go to South Africa and volunteer their time. "This was during the time when deKlerk was still president and it was very unstable. I said, 'Who would be crazy enough to go over there?' People from the U.S. were going over there and getting killed. I normally threw the journals in the trash, but I didn't throw that one away. Don't ask me why.

"That week, I don't know if this sounds strange, but the Lord spoke to me and said, 'You must go.' I said, 'Lord, you really don't need me. You don't want me to go. You better talk to whoever else is in the room,' because I didn't want to go to South Africa," she said laughing.

"Within seven weeks I was on a plane going to South Africa. I had no idea who was going to be picking me up at the airport; I just stepped out on faith.

"It was a life-altering experience. I saw almost 1,000 people in three weeks. It was just so different. I had to have my passport stamped 'Temporary White' just for me to go back and forth between cities and townships. It was just awful. It was something. It was really..." and she stopped. I didn't say anything.

"I came back from that trip and said I have got to do something. My purpose in life is not to just make people see better."

She acted on those feelings by flying to Georgetown to look into attending law school. Her goal was to practice Government and International Law and eventually change the South African constitution. "The only thing that was keeping me from going was that I couldn't sell my practice."

During that time of delay and self-analysis, she thought a lot about her life and her purpose. "It dawned on me that maybe my purpose was not only to make people see better here, but to make them see a different paradigm. To help them understand you can care about people that you've never seen before. People you think you have very little in common with until you go and you meet them and talk to them. You find out they're people just like you. With the same kind of wants, needs, hopes, goals, desires and dreams that you have.

"That was really a time when I questioned my purpose. I decided I would stay here and change people here."

Dr. Newsome changes people's paradigm in her day-to-day interactions. She also expanded her optometry building to include Advantage Learning Center, which caters to children. From time to time she shares her journey on being a trail-blazing woman and an African-American. And she volunteers her time in the Charlotte community, as well as her eye care expertise in impoverished areas around the globe.

"I do believe in God and that is such a strong influence in my life. I really do try and deal with the cards that I get dealt and go from there. I just felt South Africa was not what I was supposed to do at that time and I accepted that. And I prepared to move on."

Dr. Newsome did not become a lawyer or try to change the South African constitution, but she went back there on other medical trips as well as to Guyana and Jamaica.

Her period of self-reflection taught her a lot. She smiled and spoke in a slow rhythm. "One of the things that works for me, and I still do this, is to get some time to myself and walk or meditate or fast and pray. Be still and listen. If you don't hear anything right that second, don't panic. Know that it will come. And when it comes, be prepared to hear it. Oftentimes we hear things, we know things, but our conscious mind tries to talk us out of that which we know.

"I encourage people not to do things because other people expect you to do them, but to follow your own voice, because we all have our own voice. I think it's so critical that you listen, slow down and don't ever doubt whatever it is that you've been given; go with it."

Dr. Newsome's voice told her that she was not supposed to change the South African constitution, but that she would make a difference by changing the perspectives of people she comes into contact with.

She is a trailblazer because, "I knew I wanted to help people." She makes an impact with her patients, with her volunteer work and with her medical trips around the world.

REWIND

- The story of Dr. Newsome speaks to perseverance and self-awareness. Initially, people didn't want to hire her and were hesitant to give her a loan, so she blazed a trail on her own. She became the first African-American female to own her own optometry practice in the state of North Carolina. Dr. Newsome not only helps people's eyesight, she also helps their hearts see others more clearly.

- A lot us think we have to move to distant lands to make a difference. Yes, you can do it that way. Dr. Newsome met Nelson Mandela and started down the path of working in South Africa. But she eventually decided she could make a difference right where she was.

Wherever you are, you can change the world by being a positive role model and changing the paradigms of the people you come into contact with.

CHAPTER THIRTY-THREE

If You Love It, You Won't Stop

87 years old and still working (by choice)

This chapter truly epitomizes what happens when you love your job: It won't matter if you spend 84,000 or 104,000 hours doing it. You won't want to stop working.

In Houma, Louisiana, I spent the night at the home of 87-year-old financial planner, Jim Gueydan and his wife, Grace. One of my fraternity brothers connected me to "Mr. G." He told me, "You've got to meet this guy."

When I arrived in Houma, Mr. G was at work, so I went to his Legg Mason financial planning office. His hair shone silver, in contrast to his dark suit. We exchanged pleasantries and then I followed his Cadillac to a sprawling ranch home, which I later learned was 5,000 square feet. It had pillars in the front and a golf course for a backyard.

Mr. G finished up some work, changed into shorts and took me on a tour of Houma, a parish of 100,000. Houma is right on the Gulf of Mexico. Their main economic drivers are energy and the growing Cardiovascular Institute of the South. We drove past many companies built around oil. I saw nearly-completed super structures of oil rigs that would eventually be sunk and welded into the Gulf. Mr. G explained the history of Houma and took me to see eight mammoth blimp slips that were used for water surveillance patrols in World War II.

Over the two hours that our tour lasted, I told myself there was no way I was sitting with an 87-year-old. In the car our conversation flowed freely, just a chat between new friends. We covered a wide range of topics: politics, warfare, Iraq, investments and what I learned to be his favorite, education. "Andrew, the national government system requires an educated electorate, which we no longer have. We have social promotions."

The only conversational clue to his age was mention of the arthritis that doesn't allow him to turn his head fully. Peacefulness and wisdom exuded from Mr. G as we pulled into his driveway. "It's time to have a libation on the patio. We make what we think is a pretty good gin and tonic. What do you think?" he asked with a smile.

After a few minutes Mr. G, Grace and I sat with our drinks in their screened patio that was about the size of a rectangular, in-ground swimming pool. The music of a waterfall fountain harmonized with the sounds of a golf course at dusk.

Grace was just as warm and friendly as Mr. G. She greeted us upon our return from the tour in a pink jumpsuit and announced that a roast was in the oven. I could tell they were both very happy as they needled each other playfully.

When it came time for the interviews, Mr. G wanted Grace to go first. She had retired as Dean of Nursing at Nicholls State University. She said, "One of the things you need is a passion for what you do. You need to believe in what you do and then spend your life doing it."

Grace was the youngest of a family of eight and said she always wanted to be a nurse. She didn't read books and research it, she just knew it. "It's almost like I was destined in this world to take care of people."

At this, Mr. G chimed in, "Grace is instinctively a caregiver in everything she does."

Then he got a mischievous smile on his face. "I volunteer, you can take care of me," he said as we all laughed. Grace went in to check on the roast.

On the tour, Mr. G hadn't given me much detail on himself, but now he began to share some of his life learnings. "My philosophy, the reason I think I'm here and my central focus is that I want the life of everyone I touch to be better because I passed this way. It's as simple as that. The problem is that every person you touch has a different need," he explained.

Mr. G started his career in the Air Force. It was there he learned about honor and how to be a leader.

A life or death experience while flying a Boeing B-39 ingrained in him the need for personal integrity. As a pilot he had to rely on the ground crew to check the plane and tell him that it was ready to go. "The ground crew chief had signed off that the engine had fluid and was proper. Someone else had signed off that he had checked it, too. The thing was, they couldn't get the cap off, so they just signed off on it. I wasn't airborne very long when the red light came on. I knew if I didn't get that thing on the ground soon, the engine would seize and I'd be done. From that, I learned the need for integrity in everything you do and on the part of other people."

The Air Force honed Mr. G's business management skills during his rise from crew member to successfully managing his own B-47 squadron. He was given one of the poorer performing squadrons in SAC (Strategic Air Command). "We ended up with the best squadron and the top wing in SAC."

He attributed his success to matching people's skills to their positions. "It gets down to specifics. I told them specifically what they had to do to improve rather than chewing their butts. And then I shuffled the crews around so there was no crew with a significant weakness. With no crew with a significant weakness, we didn't have any major problems and we jumped up," he explained.

Leading up to Mr. G's retirement from the Air Force, he took an aptitude and interest test which indicated that he had equal aptitudes for sales and management. He entered the financial world as a typical stockbroker, hunting for stocks that would go up. Later, he excelled at the finance exams; they moved him to Houma in 1975 to manage the office.

He hasn't looked back. "I have people and clients with complete misunderstandings on what to do in order to be successful. You're not going to make much money buying high and selling low. My job is to get through to them and help them."

His current team has three professionals and two assistants and they manage approximately $140 million of other people's money, which is more than average. "I spend my time dealing with people who are above average in intelligence, above average in integrity and basically, nice people. That's not a bad way to live. I have a wonderful relationship with my co-workers and clients," he said with a smile.

He referred back to his reason for being here. "My philosophy for being here is that I want the life of everyone I touch to be better. Being in the financial business, there are an awful lot of people who need help."

It was then that I decided to ask a question I had wondered about since I saw his house for the first time. It seemed to me Mr. G and Grace had plenty of money to retire. "Mr. G, you don't really need to work do you?" I asked.

He shook his head and humbly said, "No. I'm working to help. "

He then talked about some of his clients. One was a recent widow who doesn't have enough money to live properly. "Inflation is going to eat up her purchasing power and she'll be destitute in 15 years. She's got a life expectancy of more than that. Her time horizon isn't next year, it's 15 or 20 years. This is a person I can help," he said as his eyes opened wider.

He told me about a girl at his office who was hired as a receptionist. She had a high school degree, was married with kids and not in a position to pay for her own college education. She was extremely bright and Mr. G saw something in her. Legg Mason reimburses their employees for half their tuition upon graduation, so he fronted her the money. She earned her college degree, became a Certified Financial Planner and is now a full-fledged member of his team. "I feel very good that I was a person who helped her move on to where she is now. She is highly qualified, extraordinarily competent and is going to have a highly successful career for the rest of her life."

Grace came back in and sat with us. Mr. G quieted down and motioned for her to continue her story. "My passions are nursing with high standards and children."

Her position at Nicholls State evolved from faculty, to department head, to dean. The interaction with the students drove her. Many students would come to her discouraged about grades, boards, finances or family issues. "If you live every day of your life to be the kind of person that you are meant to be, and you do that at home as well as at work, you will reach out and help people make choices," she said.

Now, in retirement, Grace's focus is on caring for children. She's been on the board of director's for the McDonald's Children's Service (not Ronald McDonald House) in Houma since 1986 and at the time of our conversation, chaired the board. The service serves as a residential home on 17 acres for abused and neglected children. She paused for a moment. "My life is happier and more wonderful now than it has ever been in my whole life," she flashed a big smile.

We talked about why that was the case. "I think it's sharing life with a person who you love very much. I've also accomplished a lot of my goals and now have the time to choose my own schedule and do the wonderful, peaceful things that I've always wanted to do. But a lot of my happiness comes from making the person I love happy," she said.

"See how self-centered she is," Mr. G added with a chuckle.

We sat and listened to the sounds of Mother Nature. Mr. G spoke. "Grace talked about passion. I think I'm passionate about both my occupation and my avocation, which is education."

He was the most recent president of the Federal Foundation of Academic Excellence in Public Education, which raises funds to provide individual grants to teachers and to schools that have a specific project the school board can't fund. They've donated scholarships to Nicholls State and to Mt. St. Mary's in Little Rock where his two daughters and three granddaughters went to high school. "We'll find someone that needs help in education and we'll do it quietly."

Grace went in to check on the roast again. I asked Mr. G what his secret was. He laughed for a second and thought about it. "I have been asked many, many times, what the secret is. I have thought a lot about it. First of all, you have to be in an occupation you really think is worth doing so that you enjoy going to work. If you have an occupation you enjoy, you will work at it, you will become good at it and you'll become prosperous because people will know you are good at it. If you're good at it, you don't have to bullshit. Everything tends to work out if you're good at what you do.

"The next thing, and I'll use the term relationship although I hate it, you have to be happily married. It's essential for me. I was widowed for four years and Grace had been widowed 14 years. I can tell you that the four years before I met Grace are worlds apart. No comparison. You have to have that.

"Then you have to have something beyond your occupation and a happy home life. There has to be something else outside of that, which you think is more important than you are, worthy of anything you can give it in the form of time or money or anything else. For both Grace and me, it's education. It has to be something where you don't make any money out of it. It's something that you know you have to do."

Grace called out to us that dinner was ready. Mr. G got up from his chair and chuckled, "It's time to feed the stomach instead of the soul."

The pork roast was phenomenal. We spent the rest of night discussing different points in their lives. They were both very humble and it was funny to hear them prying accomplishments out of each other.

The next morning we had breakfast before Mr. G went to work. Mr. G said with his deep laugh, "Andrew, we normally have one drink and go to bed at 10. Last night we had more than one drink and stayed up until midnight. We must have liked your company." And I truly enjoyed theirs.

REWIND

- By helping people with their finances, Mr. G is doing his part to touch as many people as possible. Even though he and Grace could be retired on a tropical island if they wanted to, his passion to help others carries him to work. Even at 87 years old.

  Mr. G is an example for all of us. When you love what you do, work is not just work. It becomes your way of life. You will not want to retire; you will just keep on going. And as Ted Benna, the founder of the 401(k), noted, our only choice may be to work longer. So wanting to keep working is a state worth wishing for.

- Mr. G's secrets to life are not a secret. We typically know these things, but living them is a different story. That is why it is great to hear the advice from a fulfilled 87-year-old:

  1. Be in an occupation you really think is worth doing so that you enjoy going to work.

  2. Be in a happy relationship.

  3. Find something outside of work and home that you think is more important than you are.

CHAPTER THIRTY-FOUR

Having an Impact
A teacher's body slam

This last interview chapter includes some of my own personal history. During my high school days at Greece Olympia in a suburb of Rochester, New York, you might say I was social. As a senior, I was given the ever-prestigious title of Class Partier, which is sure to lead to success. One teacher from those days, Mr. Armocida (Mr. A), left a mark on me. Initially, his mark was bruised shoulder blades from having been body-slammed against an unforgiving, thick wooden door.

That day was not unlike many of my senior year. I had already been accepted to college, so I focused my efforts on friends, girls and parties. The school year had just started and one of my friends who had graduated the year before picked me up from school. It was a nice September day and we drove to a park. An hour later he dropped me back at school just in time for Mr. A's fifth-period class. I was not sober. My eyes were red as blood, a slanted smile was plastered on my face and the smell of patchouli emanated from my clothes.

I didn't care much about my classes, but Mr. A's class was the one that we all wanted to be in. He was a teacher who related to you. Mr. A ran the business department and the bookstore, which stocked and sold candy. He also ran DECA, a marketing team that competed, and usually won, at statewide competitions each year.

I looked forward to the class both because of Mr. A and because it boasted a large cast of pretty girls. I floated into the room, glassy eyed and smiley, and took my customary spot in the center of the back row.

Mr. A was short, stocky and obviously Italian. He was from Long Island and let us know about it. His dark hair and black mustache were never out of place and he usually wore a blue, button-down collared shirt. Class began and I was on fire with comments and insight. The class

laughed at my wit. I couldn't tell you the subject of that day's class, just that I was very vocal. The class flew by and the bell rang. Mr. A asked me to stay after, which was not unusual because we had a friendly relationship.

The class filed out. He led me into the bookstore, but the sliding flip-top door was down. The candy store was closed. The latch on the door we had entered through clicked shut. There was silence as he made eye contact with me. He stared at me. I was paranoid and tried to avoid his locked eyes. "What are you doing?" he asked in a quiet tone.

"Nothing, I thought it was a good class," I said and grinned.

"Look at you. Look at your eyes. What's going on?"

I shifted my weight and stared at the floor. "Nothing. Nothing's going on. My allergies have been acting up," I said.

"Don't you lie to me, Andy! What are you doing?"

I looked at him. "Nothing Mr. A, I swear."

With that, he put his hands in my arm pits and half-carried me across the bookstore. Slam! I crashed against the heavy, storage room door. It did not budge. The air whooshed out of me. He set me down and got nose-to-nose with me. "Don't you lie to me. Don't you lie to me," he said with a finger poking into my chest.

"You're stoned! You've been smoking pot. I can tell."

He continued to grill me and it wasn't long before I broke down. He knew I was high and there was no way of getting around it. He was not a teacher you could bullshit. Tears began to run down my cheeks. I was a party guy on the outside, but a wuss on the inside. "What are you doing? I just don't get it. C'mon, And (his shortened nickname for me)."

A student knocked on the bookstore door. He told them to wait. We remained there for ten minutes. He talked and I listened. My buzz had been slammed off of me. "Don't you ever, ever let me see you like this again," he said, as I sniffled and tried to regain my composure.

Other teachers knew what I had been doing, but Mr. A was the only one to call me on it. Back then I was invincible, so I didn't stop my partying. It crushed my parents. It got me booted off the basketball team as well as a branded, self-inflicted tattoo. I didn't take action on what Mr. A said that day, but I always remembered it.

As I traveled and conducted my interviews, I remembered Mr. A's passion and wanted to reconnect with him. I wanted to tell him that his caring and his effort in taking action left a lasting impression on me. I wanted to thank him.

When we met for lunch at the Applebee's in Webster, New York, it had been 11 years since we'd seen each other. It was summertime and he wore an untucked maroon golf shirt. His hair and mustache had grayed, but he was as intense and energetic as ever. "Andy Harrison. How the hell are ya?" he asked.

Mr. A was now the principal of a middle school in Wayne County. The DECA program he had built at Olympia was tops in the state for 12 years, but it dissolved three years after he left to take the principal's job. We reflected on a lot of the kids who had attended school with me and I gave him updates on some of them. Though Mr. A had his own son and daughter, he still found the time to truly care for his students. He was always so passionate and intense, sometimes bordering on psycho (a word he liked to use). "I just had great kids. I treated you guys like you were my own. I didn't realize how unique that was. I just did what I did because I thought it was the right thing to do."

He loved the DECA competitions because it gave people a chance for recognition. Being in the hunt for state championships over 12 years allowed for some great times. "I wanted everyone to feel that moment of success when they hear their name and get something tangible, not just a good grade. When somebody gives you an award, for that one moment in time, there is no doubt you are the best at what you do. It's not debatable. Those occasions happen so rarely in somebody's life."

He smiled as he thought back. "I would watch them as they heard their names called, I'd watch them get those awards and I'd watch their smiles. Those kids' feet weren't touching the ground. It was always about the kids. I wanted them to experience that recognition. I never had that experience but knew what it could mean to those kids."

Our food came and he talked about his schooling. "When I was a kid, I never had a teacher I liked. No one took the time to say, 'You're a good kid,' or, 'You're screwing up.' You know, 'I'm paying attention to you.'"

I told him that was why I called him, because he was the only teacher who told me I was screwing up. He laughed. "You were on the fence there, my friend. I always saw you as a kid with tremendous potential. Really, you were a bright kid. But you are one of the lucky ones. I have seen kids throw their lives away." There was a brief silence. I was picturing some of my friends from the past. Some were dead. Some were still messed up.

Mr. A got into teaching in a roundabout way. "My grandfather taught me about education. He came over to the U.S. 'on the boat' and because he couldn't speak English, he couldn't get a job. He used to shovel snow in front of Brooklyn schools for 25 cents an hour."

Mr. A's father, aunts and uncles attended the schools where his grandfather worked. "My grandfather told us you have a choice in your life. 'You can use your back or you can use your brain. Look at me, I used my back. Use your brain!' There was always this push that education was the neutralizer in any culture. No matter where you came from, if you're educated you can do so many things."

But Mr. A didn't see teaching as part of his career path. Coming from a family of six kids where his dad worked and mom stayed at home, Mr. A didn't have a lot of material things growing up. The other kids at school rubbed it in his face and he saw that the only way to nice things was through money. He chuckled. "My goal was to be a millionaire by the time I was 25."

He went to the University of Buffalo as a business major. During his sophomore year, he was working on a group presentation with people who were majoring in education. After the presentation they told him he should really consider becoming a teacher. "I'm like, 'What are you talking about? Don't walk up to me with that crap. Do you know what those people go through? I hated my teachers. I'm not one of those dorks,'" he chuckled.

His peers saw something in his personality. After some thought, he started taking education classes and instantly enjoyed them. His wife, Nancy, told him that his large family had exposed him to kids his whole life and that gave him the ability to relate so well. "I told her the reason I tried to relate to kids was because when I was a kid, adults didn't relate to me. I wasn't the brightest kid in the class, I wasn't a star athlete or the best looking kid, and not being Irish at a parochial school didn't help. I never got anything from my teachers. Not one of them told me, 'You can do anything. If you work hard, I'll help you.' I never heard that."

Mr. A smiled as he confided that he hadn't become a millionaire by age 25. He received his degree in business education and at the time of our interview, had been in education for 28 years. "I've had very intense relationships with the kids I taught. They were extended family."

As a principal, the day-to-day interaction is different than that of a teacher, but his goals have not changed. When he has been working in his office too long, he heads to the cafeteria or the halls. He tells his secretary as he leaves, "I need a kid fix."

I asked him if the students have changed from when I was in school. Without hesitation he replied, "Kids will always be kids. Kids want somebody to care for them. They want somebody to tell them that they're OK. They want someone to say, 'I'm going to protect you and I'm not going to hurt you and I'm not going to let anybody else hurt you.' If kids receive that message, regardless of the venue, then they'll respond appropriately."

He smiled his psycho smile. "You become a teacher because you love kids and you feel like you can make a difference in their lives. I always want to have an impact."

• • • • • • • • • • • • • • •

REWIND

- I think we all want to have an impact, but we don't always know how. Sometimes it takes others to suggest a path for us. Mr. A was planning on going into business until the students in a college work group suggested that he'd be a good teacher. They were right.

- Mr. A shows us how making a difference in other people's lives can give us purpose and passion for our own. Even after 28 years on the job, Mr. A is still fired up about his kids. If you care about something, you can pour your passion and intensity into it. This will cause people to respond positively. It is a win for you and for those around you.

On the days when the fire might be flickering and you question why you are putting other people ahead of yourself, take a breath and realize: we have no idea how or when our impact is being felt. Who knows, you may get a call from someone 11 years later thanking you for the impact you had on their life.

SUMMARY
Dream It, Live It!

There is a reason you have read this book. I don't know what it is. You may not know what it is. But more than likely there is something going on in your life that is similar to the way I felt in the book's introduction and first chapter—that something is missing.

Whatever your reason for reading; your time is now. The past is the past. Learn from your experiences, but don't let them define you. Today is a new day. It's time to take action. If there is something missing in your life, you can do something about it.

After meeting my interviewees and being personally transformed by their stories, I can confidently say that we all have a dream. Some of us are listening to it and trying to act on it; others have pushed their dream down. As Vic Johnson explained in Chapter 20, "Benjamin Franklin wrote that most people die at 25 and we bury their bodies 40 years later. Living life without a dream has a huge, huge impact... You've got to have a dream to have a dream come true."

In order to find out what is missing in your life, in order to live your dream, you need to listen to the feelings inside of you. Then you need to do something about it.

To help what you have learned sink in and as you ponder your next move, read this brief recap of the 11 Lessons on the road to loving your 84,000 hours at work:

Lesson One
Debunking the Work Myth

Know that without a shadow of a doubt there are people who love their jobs. Then believe that you can be one of them.

Fred Story, the music composer, was faced with a daunting question: "So if you knew you had only so long to live what would you do for the rest of your time?" He loved his work so much that when he thought he was going to die, he wanted to go to the studio and make as much music as he could.

Terri Wardlow, the guidance counselor and teacher, lives with purpose and passion by helping students. There is no question she loves her work. "I look at this not as a job but as my vocation. It's who I am. It's what I do."

Lesson Two
The Ripple Effect

When you are living with purpose and passion, your Ripple Effect can be an incredibly positive one for you and for those you come into contact with. Yet, if you work at a job you dread, your Ripple Effect will more likely be a negative one.

For Geoff Calkins, the sports columnist, and for Charlie Hinton, the lawyer turned advocate, a dissatisfied work life spawned bouts of personal depression. But once they assessed where they were and made some changes, the effect on them, for the better, was incredible. Geoff says, "I can't explain how much fun my job is now. If I won Powerball, I'd show up for work the next day."

And Charlie found his calling by helping others battle depression. Remember what Charlie said about your tombstone, "The dash in the middle is really your whole life and who you are."

Lesson Three
You Are The One

In order to live your dream, you have to take ownership and personal accountability. You have the power.

Professor Emeritus Dr. Bud La Londe told us that we have control of our work. "It's all about managing your own life. It's like being an entrepreneur, but an intellectual entrepreneur."

Natalie Bongiorno, the clinical drug research coordinator, said, "Quit complaining and actually do something about it. If you don't take the initiative to do it, there is no one else to blame."

And Kevin Harrison, the artist, explained, "You have to find your own reasons to believe."

Lesson Four
Who Are You?

If you don't know what you want to do, you need to take the steps to analyze what motivates you and what doesn't. You need to ask questions about yourself and listen to the answers.

Rosemary Haefner, the VP of HR of CareerBuilder, advised, "I would encourage people to do self-actualization activities at all points of their career. People should be realistic. You're probably not going to crack that code and figure it all out on the first try. And you know what? That's okay."

Bob Ford, the retired police chief and current college professor, tells his students, "You've got to tie a job to your personality. The focus is to clearly understand what the hell you like to do and what you don't like to do."

Lisa Caynor, a missionary, discussed using your skills to the fullest, "Don't take what you've been given; your abilities, your talents, your love, whatever it is; don't take what you've been given and bury it."

Lesson Five
Travel Your Own Road

When it comes to careers, we each have our own fingerprint. We will be faced with forks in the road. As the driver, you will need to decide between what you want to do (internal motivation) and what society, money or others think you should do (external motivation).

Brad VanAuken, the branding guru, imparted these words of wisdom, "Sometimes you're asked to be obedient to things that make no sense. I question that. Rather than being obedient, be authentic. Be the person you were meant to be and follow the spirit within you."

Pete Campbell, the shingler in Martha's Vineyard, showed us we can march to our own drum. "No worries, Bro."

Paul Mapes, the apartment maintenance man with a degree in aerospace engineering, exemplified that titles on a business card are not important. "I like fixing things. The hands-on is great. I like the autonomy. I know if I fix it, it's going to be done right."

Mary Ann Giglio, the office manager to CEOs, typifies, "Work is like life. You get out what you put into it."

Lesson Six
Opportunities Will Knock

In everyone's journey, opportunities will present themselves. At the same time, these opportunities do not jump up and down in front of us shouting that they are there. Are you open to an opportunity? What do you do when there is a roadblock? What happens when you are supposedly stuck? When you see a door begin to open, kick it in.

Dennis Wardlow, the former mayor of Key West, FL, explained, "If you worry about failure, you might as well grab a tent somewhere and sit in it because everybody is going to fail. Failure is only if you don't try."

Brooke Priddy, the dress shop owner, said, "It takes a great risk to make a great leap."

The two brothers from Vietnam lived their version of the American Dream by creating their own opportunities.

Carlos Hernandez, a cut-back employee turned social media advisor, explained, "I've had to make some lifestyle changes, but I am so much happier and more fulfilled. When I put in a good day's work, I feel so used up, but in a very good way. It is extremely satisfying."

Lesson Seven
Don't Go It Alone

The career journey is not an easy one. There is no magic pill or success formula. That's why you need other people to help you on the road. People want to help, but you have to ask.

Vic Johnson, the author and motivational speaker, suggested, "You are the same today as you'll be in five years except for two things: the books you read and the people you associate with."

Judy Williamson, the director of the Napoleon Hill World Learning Center, said, "When likeminded people come together for a common purpose they can solve many problems."

When you are on the road with a spouse, try your best to be a united team.

Glenn and Virginia Riffle, the couple who had been married for 53 years, counseled, "Married life is a 100/100, not 50/50."

Alec, the strip club manager, and his wife exemplify trust and partnership. "My wife got me this job. She hasn't worked since I started here. It's nice she can spend time at home with the kids."

Lesson Eight
To Change...

If you are thinking about making a career change, know that a switch is not easy, but it is totally acceptable. And it can lead to your purpose and passion.

Dr. Mary Cleave, the astronaut, offered a unique perspective. "Goals are great, but you need to leave your options open. Don't get trapped in them. You want to keep your eyes open because there may be something peripherally out there that's even better."

Fernan Cepero left his "dream job" as an anthropologist and eventually found his niche in human resources. Making a change is never easy, especially when you have spent years of your life in a field. "It's almost self-shock. I can't believe I am saying this to myself. I can't believe I don't want to do this."

Dr. Hillary Beberman left a cushy job at Bloomberg to go to medical school. Before she left, she asked, "Is this what I want to be doing for 50 years?" Now she recommends, "If there is something you are really unhappy doing, cut your losses."

Lesson Nine
Or Not To Change

If you have always known what you want to do, listen to yourself and go for it.

Dr. Daniel Marion, the tree pathologist, gave his success points, "It's the PDD: the persistence, the drive, and the determination."

Mary Cameron ("M.C.") VanGraafeiland, a senior publicist for Warner Brothers studios, took her own advice. "If it's something you want do, then paying your dues is worth it. If you're excited about it and you're motivated and energized, that's the real payoff."

Ted Benna, the father of the 401(k) program, almost left his field, but stuck with it and ended up having an influence on millions of people. "I've been able to do what I wanted, but do it in a different way than I thought."

Lesson Ten
How Bad Do You Want It?

To live with purpose and passion, you will likely be faced with trials and tribulations. This may cause you to question your choices. You may have to sacrifice. You may have to take risks. And you may have to blaze a new trail. But in the end, if you want it bad enough, it's all worth it.

Len and Judy Wiltberger, the winery owners who spent over 30 years making their dream a reality, explained, "You have to balance it all out. Within your restraints, you make the best choices. We didn't go full force, full time... We did what we could when we could."

Roger Bachman, the charter yacht owner, took a $500,000 gamble on his vision. "You have to know in your heart it's the right thing to do. You have to be passionate and you have to be willing to risk everything in order to do it. Are you 100 percent sure that this is the right thing to do? If you can answer that and you're willing to commit yourself to that kind of a risk, then by all means go for it."

Betty Dickey, the first ever female Chief Justice of the State Supreme Court of Arkansas, counseled, "If you don't see a problem that needs to be fixed, or a cause that's worth taking on or an adventure worth taking, you're going to look back and be very unhappy."

Lesson Eleven
Make a Difference

And finally, to live your purpose and passion, make a difference in people's lives besides your own. It is important to remember that you don't have to cure cancer to make this difference. If you love what you do, whatever it is, your Ripple Effect will be felt in a powerful way by you and by those around you.

Joe Merritt, the firefighter, medic and first responder to the 9/11 attacks on the Pentagon detailed, "I have the opportunity to get up every day and come and help people. I don't know how I could do another job."

Dr. Paula Newsome, the first African-American female to own her own optometry practice in North Carolina, saw something in herself. "I knew I wanted to help people. I encourage people to not do things because other people expect you to do them, but to follow your own voice, because we all have our own voice. My purpose was not only to make people see better here, but to make them see a different paradigm."

Jim Guedyan, the financially well-off 87-year-old financial planner, still works every day. "The reason I think I'm here and my central focus is that I want the life of everyone I touch to be better because I passed this way."

Bob Armocida, my former high school teacher, described, "You become a teacher because you love kids and you feel like you can make a difference in their lives. I always want to have an impact."

As we conclude, I am honored that you have taken time out of your life to read this book. These pages are a culmination of years of contemplation and effort. My journey has had peaks and valleys. It has had times of great joy and of painful questioning. And for all of the sacrifices that were made, I can say it was all worth it.

When I quit my job to travel the country interviewing passionate people, I had no idea what I would find. What I found was me. My mission is to inspire people—through my story and the stories of the people I was fortunate enough to interview—to work at a job they love. My job is to be a conduit to the passionate. To encourage people to give themselves permission to live their dreams. And to help others find what is missing.

The journey to loving your 84,000 hours at work is neither short nor easy. But it is a journey you need to embark on. Loving your work will be great for you and for those around you. The more of us there are on the road, the better society becomes. The world needs your positive Ripple Effect.

By reading this book, we are now on the road together; the road to loving our 84,000 hours at work. I am not a coach or a guru; I am just a guy who felt called to find what was missing and then share it with others. I will continue my journey by sharing the stories of passionate people. And who knows, maybe I'll be sharing your story one day.

Thanks for reading. I hope to see you on the road...

• • • • • • • • • • • • • • • • •

To learn more about my journey and the interviewees, or get other inspirational information and updates, please visit:

www.84000hours.com
www.iamontheroad.com